HOW TO MAKE YOUR OWN
LAMPS AND
LAMPSHADES

No. 1112
$9.95

HOW TO MAKE YOUR OWN
LAMPS AND
LAMPSHADES

BY BRUCE MITTON

TAB BOOKS
BLUE RIDGE SUMMIT, PA. 17214

FIRST EDITION

FIRST PRINTING—FEBRUARY 1979

Copyright © 1979 by TAB BOOKS

Printed in the United States of America

Library of Congress Cataloging in Publication Data

Mitton, Bruce H., 1950-
   How to make your own lamps & lampshades.

   Includes index.
   1. Lamps. 2. Lampshades. I. Title.
TT897.1.M57   745.59'32   78-26320
ISBN 0-8306-9842-6
ISBN 0-8306-1112-6 pbk.

Contents

Introduction

Good lighting is a way of life. It enables us to see and use our own personal environment, as well as the world around us. Right this minute as you read these words the value of light is apparent. Without light there would be little to see.

No longer do we have to rely on candles or kerosene and oil to supply inadequate light. Today, candles and fuel-burning lamps are a touch of antiquity used mainly to enhance mood or to be decorative.

Electricity sparked the power needed for the lighting we now take for granted. Good lighting fills our schools, shopping centers, businesses and homes. Usually the light is unobtrusive, coming from fluorescent tubes recessed in ceilings or from incandescent bulbs in light fixtures.

In our homes additional lighting is placed where it's needed. A flick of a switch can add light next to a chair for reading, on a table in a dark corner and in many other places that need to be lighted. The light comes from an incandescent bulb. That bulb is part of a decorative and functional piece of furniture called a lamp.

This book deals with light-producing lamps. Lamps that are both functional in their lighting ability and decorative for different home decors. Even more important, the lamps easily can be constructed by anyone who is willing to take the time to build his own distinctive lamps.

There's no denying that lamps of all types easily can be purchased already made. Some are expensive, others quite reasonable, depending on what type of lamp you need or want.

If you are willing to make your own lamps, you are creating a piece of functional furniture that is unique to your own personal environment. The cost is reasonable and basic lamp parts are readily available.

This is an idea book. A book that not only instructs and illustrates ways to make lamps but may spark your imagination so you can construct lamps from almost anything you have a mind to.

You don't have to make all the lamps illustrated in this book. But they serve as visual ideas and instructional aids to show you how simple lamp making can be.

Surprisingly, there are very few tools required to build lamps. Those that are needed are easy to use. You may already have many of the tools on hand if you do your own home repair.

If you have never made anything before and have the feeling you can't build a lamp, get rid of that doubt quickly by constructing the first lamp project in this book. Once you have all the materials for building this lamp, it can be constructed without tools in less than five minutes. Lamp making can't be much simpler than that.

Lamp making is like constructing a jigsaw puzzle. It's a matter of putting the pieces together correctly. Once you've read the first chapter of this book, you will know where the pieces go to the puzzle.

Bruce Mitton

Parts You Need to Make a Lamp

Before you start making your own lamps, it's necessary to familiarize yourself with the actual parts needed for lamp construction. On the next few pages we'll take a look at lamp parts and learn their function starting at the top of a common table lamp and working down to the electrical plug. Figure 1-1 shows all the parts that go together to make a lamp. Figure 1-2 shows the parts after they're put together.

THE FINIAL

Finials are the crowning touch to many lamps. They are nothing more than a decorative piece that is screwed into place to hold the lampshade on the lamp.

There are many different finials to choose from as shown in Fig. 1-3. They can be decorative brass, wood, plastic or a combination of glass and metal. Small finials are referred to as knobs.

Not all lamps need a finial or knob. It depends on the type of lampshade you are using and whether the harp has the necessary threads to hold a finial.

THE HARP

A brass or brass-plated *harp* is the support for the lampshade. They come in many sizes but there are four basic types. The most commonly used is the two-piece detachable harp which is 11 to 15 inches in height (Fig. 1-4).

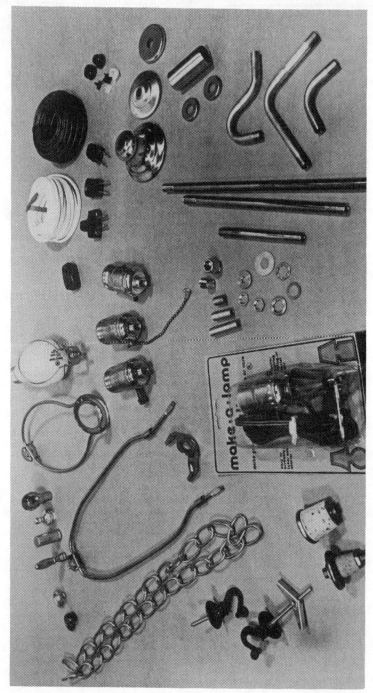

Fig. 1-1. All the parts that go together to make a lamp.

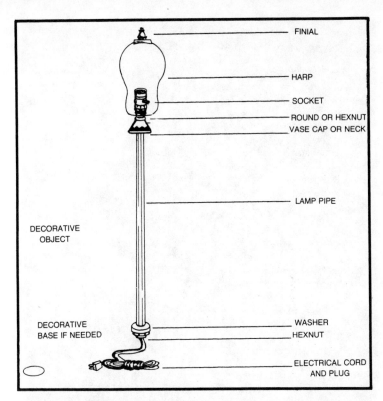

Fig. 1-2. Diagram of the parts of a lamp.

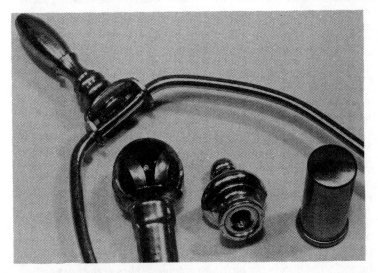

Fig. 1-3. Examples of lamp knobs and finials.

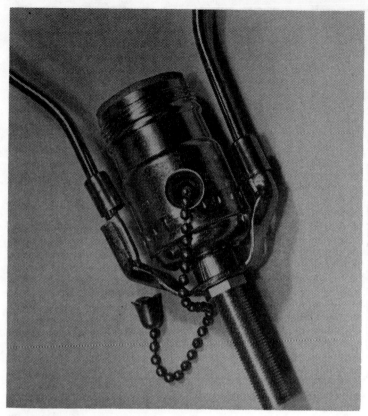

Fig. 1-4. A detachable harp assembly held in place by the light socket base and a hexnut.

Another type of harp screws onto the top of a light socket. They are usually for lamps using small lampshades.

For very small lamps there are bulb-fitting harps. These slide over the light bulb. Often, bulb fitting harps are built into commercial lampshades (Fig. 1-5).

One last harp to look for, if you're indecisive about the proper size, is an adjustable harp. It can be raised and lowered to fit many different sized lampshades.

LIGHT SOCKETS

The *light socket* holds the bulb. The difference in sockets is the on/off mechanism. The switch can be a pull chain, a small arm that is pushed from one side to the other or a knob that is turned. The turned knob sockets can be for one intensity bulbs or they can be the

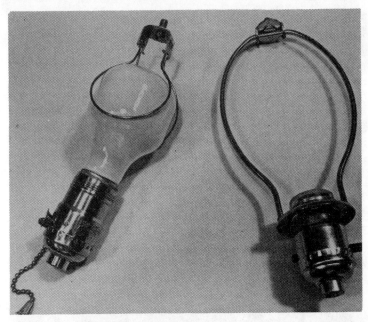

Fig. 1-5. A harp that attaches to the light bulb, left, and one that screws into the top of the light socket, right.

three-way turn knobs that are used for three-way bulbs that give different intensities of light (Fig. 1-6).

One of the newest types of light socket has a dimmer switch that is turned to control the amount of electrical current going to the

Fig. 1-6. Brass turnknob, pull chain, and push switch sockets.

Fig. 1-7. A dimmer switch socket that controls the intensity of a light bulb.

light bulb. Dimmer switch sockets are the most expensive (Fig. 1-7).

Another type of socket you may find useful in your lamp construction is the candle socket used in candelabras (Fig. 1-8).

These sockets are covered with a plastic sheath that gives the appearance of a candle. The plastic sheaths can be trimmed to the necessary size. Some candle sockets are adjustable from 3-¼ inches to 4-¾ inches (Fig. 1-9).

When constructing lamps you will be taking sockets apart to attach the electrical cord. To take a socket apart it's necessary to push with your thumb at a point near the base of the socket. Look closely at Fig. 1-10 and you'll see the word *press* written where you are supposed to apply pressure. At times it may seem the socket won't come apart. If you push hard enough with your thumb, it will separate.

Once you have taken the socket apart you will have a base and an outer metal sheath. Inside the sheath is a cardboard insulation and the actual light socket with two screw terminals for attaching the electrical cord. The socket has to be removed from the metal sheath to attach the electrical wires.

To get the socket back together again it's just a matter of pushing everything back in place.

NIPPLES

Nipples are small pieces of threaded steel pipe (Fig. 1-11). Their actual size is ¼, ⅜ or ½-inch diameter. The most commonly used in lamp construction is ⅜-inch diameter.

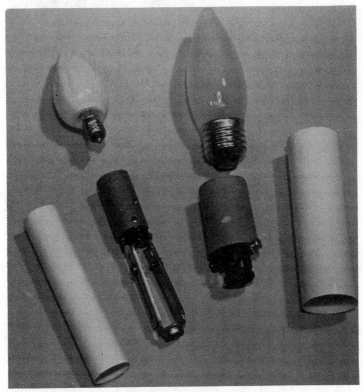

Fig. 1-8. Two candlestick sockets and their plastic sheaths.

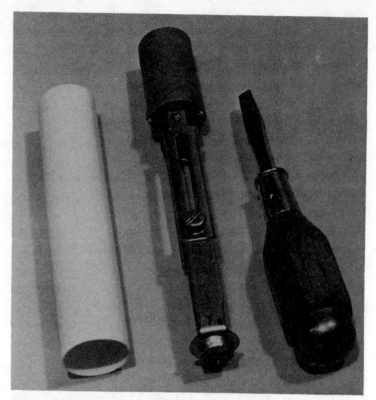

Fig. 1-9. An adjustable candlestick socket and screwdriver.

Unfortunately there can be some confusion when purchasing nipples, even though a standard has been established. Nipples are identified by the lamp industry and plumbing industry iron pipe size. The abbreviation I.P. is used. The most common nipple size used in lamp making is ⅜-inch diameter, but the nipple is referred to as ⅛-I.P. The ½-inch diameter nipples are ¼-I.P.

To avoid any confusion use ⅛-I.P. when making your lamps. It is the most commonly available. The package the nipples come in may be labeled both in the I.P. rating and as ⅜-inch diameter.

Nipples support the socket, harp, and may hold a lamp together. They come in many different lengths and once a lamp is constructed properly are invisible to the eye. Nipples are hollow to allow for electrical cord.

LAMP PIPE

Lamp pipe has been compared to the spine of the human body, the backbone of many lamps. Made of brass or brass-plated metal, lamp pipe comes in various lengths and can be totally threaded or threaded on each end only (Fig. 1-12). Like the nipples the lamp pipe is hollow so the electrical cord can pass through it.

Lamp pipe is used, as are nipples, to support the light socket and harp. The lamp pipe may also hold the lamp together. This

Fig. 1-10. A disassembled light socket consisting of a metal outer sheath, cardboard insulation, socket, and socket base. Note the word press where you apply pressure to take the socket apart.

Fig. 1-11. Threaded steel nipples.

means holding the lamp base, decorative object, socket and harp as a single piece.

The same I.P. rating that is used for nipples is also used for lamp pipe. The most commonly used is ⅜-inch diameter with the ⅛-I.P. rating (Fig. 1-13).

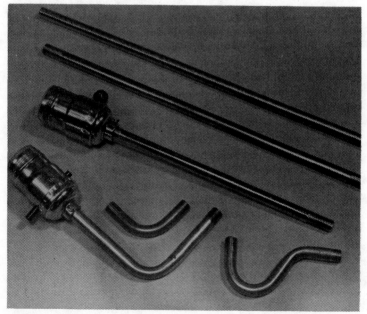

Fig. 1-12. A selection of lamp pipe.

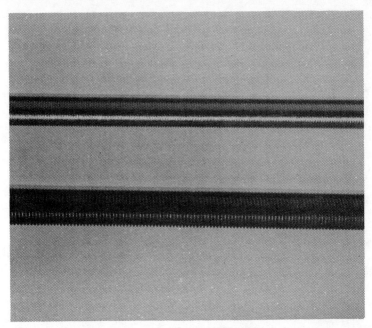

Fig. 1-13. Threaded ⅛-I.P. and ¼-I.P. lamp pipe.

As illustrated, lamp pipe can be purchased in unusual shapes, straight or curved. Each has its own specific function. Gooseneck lamp pipe is also available and is easily bent (Fig. 1-14).

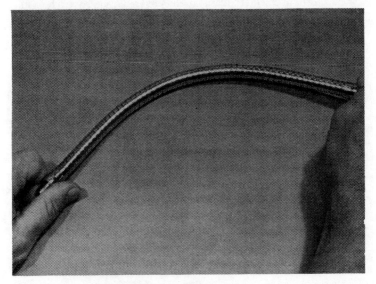

Fig. 1-14. A bendable gooseneck lamp pipe.

Fig. 1-15. Brass tops and check rings.

NECKS, SPACERS, VASE CAPS, AND TOPS

Decorative pieces of metal and sometimes wood called *necks*, *spacers*, *caps*, and *tops* are used to hide threaded nipples and lamp pipe as well as to guide and support (Fig. 1-15).

Vase caps are used to fill open ends of vases and have a hole in their center for lamp pipe to pass through. The caps come in a variety of sizes from about 1 inch to 8 inches in diameter. Vase caps are a useful part for converting many decorative objects into lamps.

Fig. 1-16. Brass neck and two check rings which guide the lamp pipe.

Fig. 1-17. An assortment of washers, and round and hex-shaped nuts.

Necks and spacers are decorative pieces that slide over lamp pipe or nipples (Fig. 1-16). They add more distinction to a lamp than just a straight piece of pipe.

WASHERS, NUTS AND COUPLINGS

With all the threads found on nipples and lamp pipe you'll need an assortment of *washers* and both round and hex-shaped *nuts*. The nuts hold many lamps together and keep lamp building parts in place (Fig. 1-17).

Couplings are small brass fittings that are used to join sections of lamp pipe or nipples together if you need an extra length of lamp

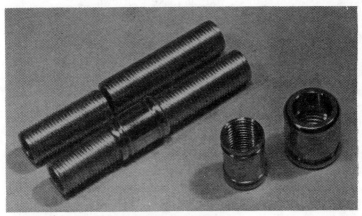

Fig. 1-18. Couplers for joining lamp pipe together.

Fig. 1-19. Rough wood bases purchased from a lumber distributor.

pipe (Fig. 1-18). The couplings are often in the interior of the lamp and are not visible when the lamp is finished.

LAMP BASES

Not all lamps will need a *base*. Those that do can have one made of wood, metal, plastic or even stone. They can be different sizes and shapes (Fig. 1-19).

Lamp bases are used when stability is needed or if a base can add decorative appeal. You can purchase lamp bases or if handy with basic woodworking tools, you can make your own.

ELECTRICAL WIRE

Electrical wire carries the current from the wall outlet to the light socket. Look for general purpose household cord. Three common colors are white, brown and black. When building lamps, some thought should be given to the cord color you are going to use (Fig. 1-20).

Generally, electrical wire won't show if it runs behind a dresser or table to the wall outlet. On occasion an electrical cord may have to run some distance along a wall to the nearest outlet.

If this is the case, it's best to use an electrical wire that is the least visible. For example, if your walls are painted white, you may want to use white cord so that it will blend in with the wall.

Six foot lengths of electrical cord are generally used for constructing lamps. For hanging lamps the electrical cord may be ten feet or longer.

ELECTRICAL CORD BUSHING INLET

You may never need electrical cord bushing *inlets*, but they can add a decorative touch if used correctly. The inlets can give a hand-crafted lamp a professional, finished look.

Inlets are made of plastic (Fig. 1-21) or metal (Fig. 1-22). They do nothing more than finish the hole the electrical cord passes through at the bottom of a lamp. Some inlets exert pressure against the wire so it can't be pulled from the lamp.

ELECTRICAL PLUGS

The final step in wiring a lamp is the addition of an *electrical plug*. The plug is inserted into the wall outlet to connect with household current.

There are several types of plugs to choose from. They come in black, brown and white. The color of the plug should be the same as the electrical wire you are using (Fig. 1-23).

Some plugs require insulation to be removed from the wire before the wires can be screwed into place. Newer plugs on the

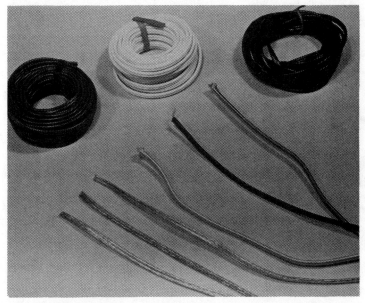

Fig. 1-20. An assortment of household electrical cord for making lamps.

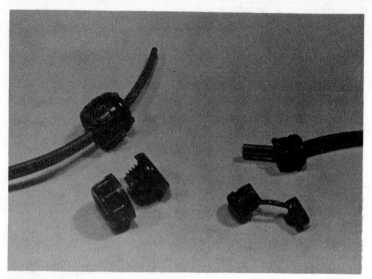

Fig. 1-21. Plastic electrical cord inlets.

market are of the quick attachment variety. No tools are required to make a good connection. The electrical wire is inserted into the plug, and by use of pressure from pulling the wire or pushing the prongs

Fig. 1-22. A brass cord inlet and hexnut.

Fig. 1-23. A screw terminal and two quick plugs.

closed, sharp points penetrate the wire's insulation making a connection (Fig. 1-24).

Quick plugs are a convenience that make plug attachment as simple as possible.

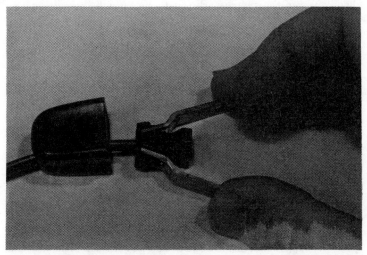

Fig. 1-24. Some quick plugs require the pushing of the prongs together to make a connection with the electrical cord.

Fig. 1-25. An in-line on/off switch.

ADDITIONAL LAMP-MAKING PARTS

We've examined the basic lamp parts needed for constructing and even repairing many different types of lighting fixtures and lamps. There are some other lamp making parts that you might find useful in your lamp construction.

In-Line On/Off Switch

For some lamps it's more convenient to have an *on/off switch* on the electrical cord. When using light sockets that have no built-in switch, it's mandatory.

A simple, very small in-line switch (Fig. 1-25) is the answer. It is easy to install. It's a matter of cutting one electrical wire, then inserting the wires into the switch mechanism and then putting the two halves of the switch back together. As with the quick plugs, small points pierce the insulation of the wire ensuring a good electrical contact (Fig. 1-26).

Lamp Adapters

Many lamp makers like to convert various glass bottles into decorative lamps. One reason is because it can be done quickly using a *lamp adapter kit* (Fig. 1-27).

The kit consists of a socket that is already wired. The wire passes through a hole in the base of the socket. Beneath the socket is a tapered piece of plastic or cork. The tapered fitting is slipped into the neck of the bottle that is to be converted into a lamp. Add a light bulb and lampshade. Bingo! You have made a lamp.

Other lamp adapters are nothing but a piece of cord with a cap on each end of the cord and a nipple running through the center.

The lamp maker has to add a socket and drill a hole through the bottom of the glassware for the electrical cord to pass through. A little more work is involved than just inserting a lamp adapter kit.

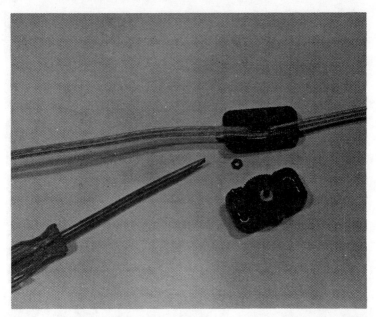

Fig. 1-26. One wire of the electrical cord has to be cut before the wire is inserted into the in-line switch mechanism.

Fig. 1-27. Two brass and cork lamp adapters and a ready-made lamp adapter kit of plastic.

Fig. 1-28. A swag hook kit and fixture chain for hanging light fixtures.

Brass Loops, Swag Hook Kit and Chain

Hanging lamps are a common sight in many homes. Usually they hang from a decorative hook in the ceiling. These hooks are called *swag hooks* and come with both a wood screw and spring toggle for installation in either wood beams or through plasterboard (Fig. 1-28).

Brass loops are used as a finishing touch, much as a finial. The difference is the loops have a hole through their center so the electrical cord can pass upward toward the ceiling (Fig. 1-29).

Hanging lamps are attached to *metal chain* and the electrical cord weaves through the chain to make it as unnoticeable as possible.

Finishing Felt

Table lamps that you make may need to be covered with a protective piece of *felt* or other material. This will protect the surface of the furniture you set your lamp on. Some materials are self-adhesive while others can be attached using one of the many glues that are available (Fig. 1-30).

Light Bulbs

Today's incandescent bulbs are at least ten times more efficient than the first practical bulb invented by Thomas Edison.

Fig. 1-29. Two loops used for hanging light fixtures.

Fig. 1-30. Felt or self-adhesive materials are used to cover the bottoms of lamps and protect furniture.

29

Fig. 1-31. An assortment of light bulbs.

Light bulbs come in many shapes, colors and sizes (Fig. 1-31). More important is the wattage or intensity of light they produce.

When selecting a bulb for your completed lamps, you want the proper wattage or intensity of light to suit the lamp's purpose. Neither too bright for a night light nor too dim for a reading light.

WHERE TO GET LAMP-MAKING PARTS

You can find most of the lamp parts you'll need in a large department store's lighting or hardware section.

Electrical supply stores and stores that specialize in selling lighting fixtures and shades also carry a wide assortment of lamp parts.

It may take some searching to find specific parts for unusual lamp-making creations. With a little ingenuity you may find substitutes for specific lamp-making parts.

Tools Used to Make a Lamp

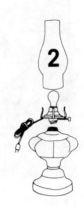

In order to make lamps you need a few tools (Fig. 2-1). Good tools are like a close friend, treat them with respect and you'll have them around a long time. I've listed each of the tools you might use in lamp construction and given reasons why you need them. Whenever possible I've listed alternative methods to keep your production costs as low as possible.

DRILLS AND BITS

Most lamps you make will require a hole or two. You'll need to drill a hole for the electrical cord inlet and a hole or two for lamp pipe or nipples which may hold the lamp together and support the light socket.

There are three types of drills to choose from. There is the *simple hand drill* for up to ¼-inch holes, the *hand-operated brace* for holes larger than ¼-inch (Fig. 2-2) and the *power drill* which comes in various sizes.

The easiest drill to use is the power drill (Fig. 2-3). Its high speed will put a hole through anything, providing you have the correct type of bit.

The brace is used for wood and is useful for drilling large 1-inch holes to countersink nuts and washers at the base of the lamp. Countersinking will hide the washers and nuts and allow the lamp to sit flat.

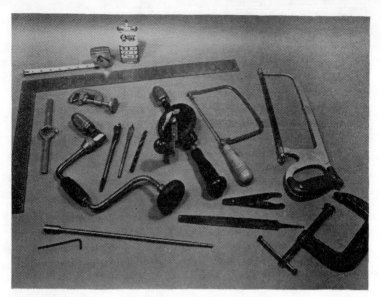

Fig. 2-1. Some common tools you'll use to make lamps.

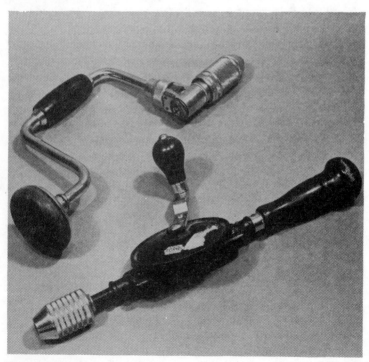

Fig. 2-2. Examples of a hand drill and brace.

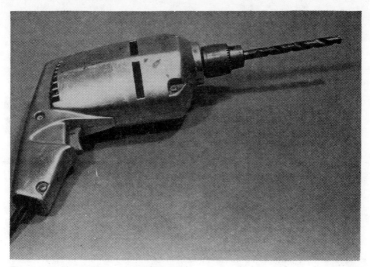

Fig. 2-3. An easy to use electrical drill.

Bits

Once you have the drilling tool, you are going to need some *bits*. The bits actually do the cutting (Fig. 2-4). Twist drills are bits designed for cutting metal, but will drill through wood also. They come in various sizes from about 1/16-inch up to ½-inch all the way to 3 inches. For counter-sinking washers and nuts you may have to drill 1-inch diameter holes.

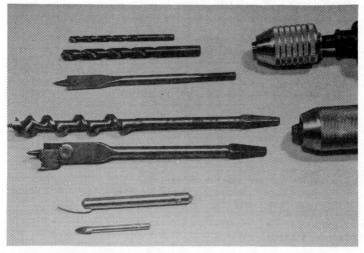

Fig. 2-4. Twist bits, wood bits for a brace, and tungsten carbide bits for drilling glass.

Fig. 2-5. Tungsten-carbide tipped masonry bits.

Your lamps will be made of wood, metal, ceramic or even glass. Glass is probably the most difficult to drill through. A special bit made of tungsten-carbide is needed. Glass is brittle material and care must be used when drilling through it.

The glass you drill through should be firmly supported in a vise or with the use of clamps. A lubricant of turpentine or kerosene is needed when drilling with tungsten-carbide bits. Practice will get you used to drilling through glass. Drill slowly and give the bits a chance to cool off every now and then.

For ceramic materials a masonry bit is used (Fig. 2-5). Masonry bits are carbide-tipped. As with glass, drilling through ceramics should be done carefully to prevent breaking and chipping.

One other drilling tool you may need is a bit extension (Fig. 2-6). These extensions are from 12 to 18 inches long and are used to drill deep holes. The holes they drill are fairly large because the bit extension needs to follow the bit you are using. For drilling long, deep holes in lamp making, this is an advantage. This allows for error. Long holes are difficult to drill straight.

Most of the bits you will be using are ⅜-inch in diameter—the same diameter as lamp pipe and nipples. You may use a smaller ¼-inch bit for holes allowing the lamp cord to pass through the bases of various objects.

Drilling Correctly

The secret to drilling any hole correctly is to hold the drill so it is perpendicular to the material you are drilling (Fig. 2-7). Try at all

34

times to keep a 90-degree angle where the bit enters the material to be drilled. Don't rush your drilling. Drill slowly and carefully.

Whenever drilling through wood, there is the chance of splintering when the bit breaks through. To prevent some of the splintering and reduce the amount of sanding you may have to do later, put a backup piece of wood on the opposite side of the wood you are drilling through. You'll actually be drilling through two pieces of wood.

It's best to have any material you drill through stationary, unable to move. That's easily accomplished by either a vise or clamps.

If you need to countersink a hole, make sure you drill the large countersink hole first to the proper depth. Then drill the smaller hole. It's very difficult to drill a large hole over a smaller hole if the bit has nothing to grip.

Drilling Safely

When drilling through glass, it's wise to wear a pair of protective gloves. There will be less chance of getting cut if the glassware you are drilling through breaks.

Anytime you are drilling, you should wear protective goggles or glasses to prevent small materials from entering your eyes.

BENCH VISE AND CLAMPS

If you are fortunate enough to have a work bench, you may want to invest in an iron *bench vise* that holds just about anything (Fig.

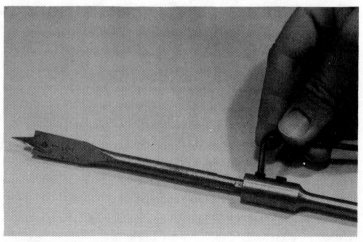

Fig. 2-6. A bit extension assembly.

Fig. 2-7. When using a drill, keep a 90-degree angle at the point the bit enters the material you are drilling.

2-8). It comes in different sizes and price range. It's simply two metal claws that open and close. Care must be taken to protect the material you are holding in the vise. The metal jaws can leave marks on wood, metal and painted surfaces.

Fig. 2-8. A heavy bench vise is a useful tool for constructing lamps.

Scrap wood or even heavy cloth can be used between the object and the metal claws of the vise to prevent any marking.

A less expensive way to hold materials in place while drilling, cutting or even sanding is by using *clamps* (Fig. 2-9). Not only will

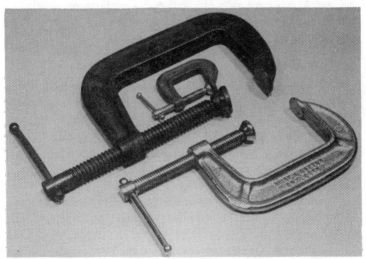

Fig. 2-9. C-clamps are inexpensive and are useful in holding objects stationary.

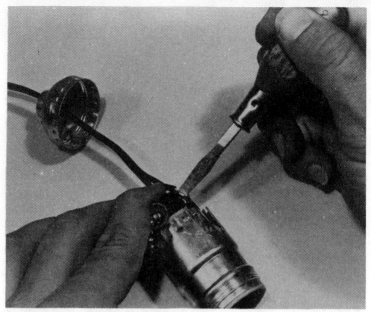

Fig. 2-10. A small, conventional flat blade screwdriver will be needed for attaching the electrical cord to the terminals of the light socket.

these metal c-shaped clamps hold materials in place but can help secure glued materials while they are drying.

C-clamps come in various sizes and are simple to use. As with a metal bench vise, c-clamps can damage or mar the material they are holding. A protective piece of wood or cloth can be inserted between the clamp and the material you are holding in place to prevent any unwanted marks.

SCREWDRIVERS

Screwdrivers are designed to tighten and loosen screws. There are two basic types, the conventional *flat blade* and the cross-slotted *Phillips*.

You'll only need a fairly small conventional screwdriver for loosening and tightening the screw terminals found on a light socket (Fig. 2-10). These screws on a socket hold the electrical wires in place.

Light sockets also have a small set screw at their bases. This screw will need to be tightened when the socket base is in place (Fig. 2-11).

In lamp making screwdrivers also are used for prying or even as chisels as they're pounded on with a hammer.

SAWS

If you plan on making your own wood bases to give an additional hand-crafted look to your lamps, you are going to need some type of saw to cut the wood.

An electrical *jigsaw* is an all-around cutting tool. You can cut straight lines as well as gradual curves to make circular wood bases.

If you don't have a jigsaw or wish to spend the money on one, you use a small inexpensive *coping saw*. It's capable of cutting straight and curved lines, too. The blade is small so you'll have to work slowly and carefully (Fig. 2-12).

A regular *cross-cut* or *rip saw* is useful for cutting quick straight lines. As the names implies, one saw is for cutting across the grain of the wood and the other is for cutting with the grain.

One saw you may need for cutting lengths of lamp pipe or nipples is a *hacksaw*. It's used strictly for cutting metal. Threaded lamp pipe is easiest to cut with the thin blade of a hacksaw (Fig. 2-13).

PIPE CUTTER

Another tool that works at cutting metal lamp pipe is a small *pipe cutter* (Fig. 2-14). It's nothing more than a small blade that is

Fig. 2-11. The screwdriver will also be used for tightening the set screw on the socket's base.

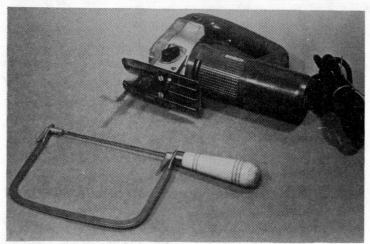

Fig. 2-12. A small coping saw and a power operated jigsaw.

screwed on to the pipe you are cutting. The cutter is rotated around the pipe, as you gradually increase the blade's pressure against the pipe (Fig. 2-15). A good pipe cutter will cut a straight line. Use a pipe cutter only on unthreaded pipe for best results.

You can purchase lamp pipe cut to specific sizes which will fit many different lamps. If you use ready-cut lamp pipe, you may not need either the hacksaw or pipe cutter.

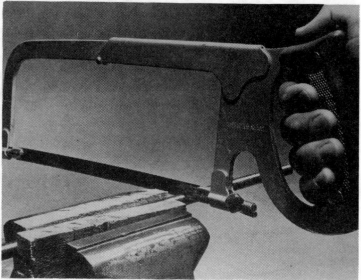

Fig. 2-13. A hacksaw is useful for cutting lamp pipe to the proper length.

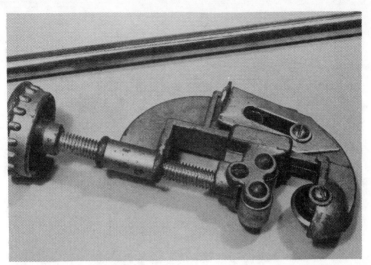

Fig. 2-14. An easy-to-use pipe cutter.

You may not need any saw if you plan to purchase already-cut wood bases. Some hobby and wood supply stores supply small wood bases that can be used in lamp construction. Some specialty stores sell ready-made lamp bases of wood and metal.

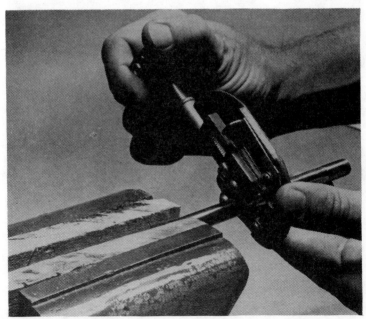

Fig. 2-15. Pipe cutters should be used on unthreaded lamp pipe only.

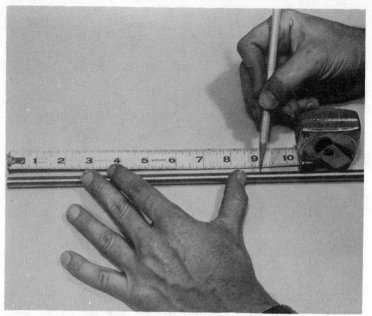

Fig. 2-16. A tape measure is a useful tool for measuring lamp pipe.

MEASURING DEVICES

It's important that you have a measuring device on hand. This can be a *ruler*, *yardstick*, *tape measure* or a good *square*. You'll need to measure the lamp pipe (Fig. 2-16), electrical cord, wood bases (Fig. 2-17) and even some of the brass fittings.

Fig. 2-17. A metal square is used in measuring wood bases for your lamps.

DIE AND DIE STOCK HOLDER

Occasionally you may find it necessary to thread your own lamp pipe. If you do, you'll need a *die* and *die holder* (Fig. 2-18). A ⅛-inch die threads pipe for the socket, nuts and other lamp making materials (Fig. 2-19).

When threading pipe you need plenty of good lubricating oil. Pipe must be held firmly in place or it's very hard to thread (Fig. 2-20).

OPEN END WRENCH

A ½-inch *open-end wrench* (Fig. 2-21) will be needed to tighten hex-shaped nuts that are used to hold pieces of the lamp together (Fig. 2-22). Pliers will also work.

When countersinking washers and nuts, it's best to use a socket wrench that can fit into a one-inch hole where an open-end wrench won't reach.

MISCELLANEOUS TOOLS

In the following group, I'll throw in anything I think you may need or tools that can make lamp making easier. You can use your own judgment whether to invest in the tool or not.

Wire Stripper

The *wire stripper* (Fig. 2-23) is a simple tool used to peel away insulation from electrical cord. It's quick, easy, and accurate (Fig.

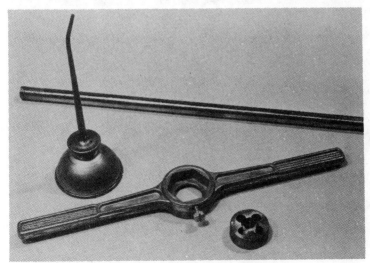

Fig. 2-18. A die and die stock holder for threading lamp pipe.

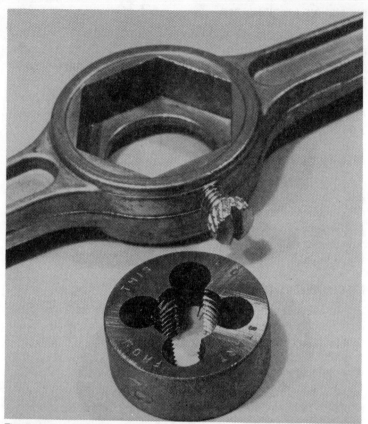

Fig. 2-19. The threading die tells you which side to start from.

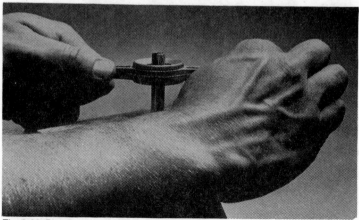

Fig. 2-20. Pipe that is to be threaded needs to be held firmly in place and plenty of lubricating oil needs to be used.

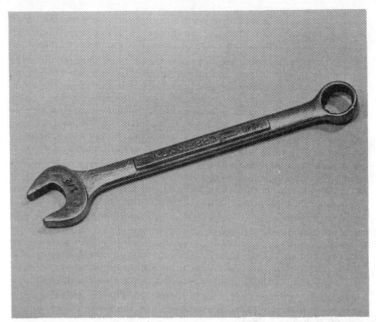

Fig. 2-21. An open-end wrench.

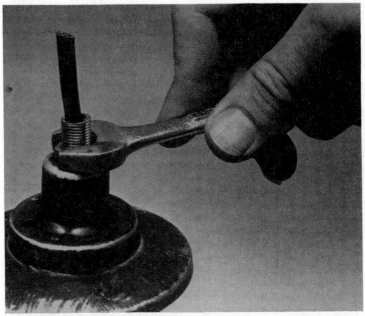

Fig. 2-22. The open-end wrench will be used to tighten hexnuts during lamp assembly.

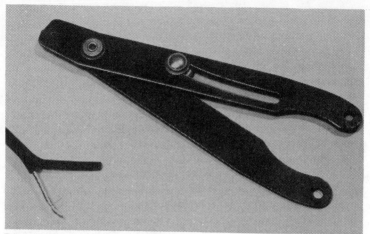

Fig. 2-23. An inexpensive wire stripper.

2-24). A sharp knife can peel away the insulation, too, but care must be taken not to cut the fine copper wires beneath the insulation.

Soldering Iron and Solder

Soldered wire (Fig. 2-25) ensures a good electrical connection. Most of the lamp making wire connections are held in place by a small retaining screw. The ends of stripped wire can be *soldered* to keep the many small copper wires together and to make it easier to wrap them around the retaining screws before tightening (Fig. 2-26).

Fig. 2-24. A wire stripper can make quick and accurate removal of insulation.

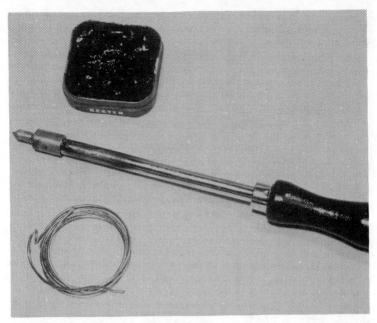

Fig. 2-25. A soldering iron, solder and flux.

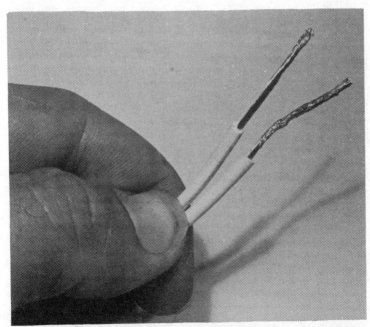

Fig. 2-26. Soldered wires are easier to work with and ensure a good electrical contact with the light socket.

47

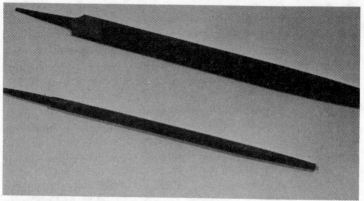

Fig. 2-27. Round or flat files are useful in lamp construction.

File

A round or flat *file* may be useful in removing burrs from cut lamp pipe or enlarging holes for wire or lamp pipe to pass through (Fig. 2-27).

Wood Finishing Tools

If you plan to make your own decorative wood bases, you will need some wood finishing materials. This includes different grades

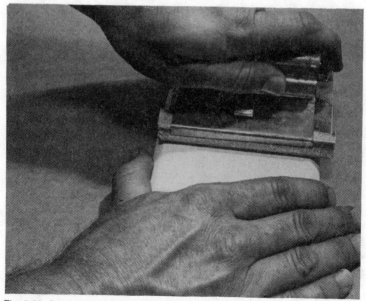

Fig. 2-28. Sandpaper and a sanding block make finishing wood bases easier.

of *sandpaper*, from coarse to very fine grit and, of course, either *paint* or *stains* for adding the color you desire.

A small *sanding block* will make sanding easier (Fig. 2-28). This can be purchased or you can use a small piece of wood with the sandpaper wrapped around it.

If you plan on rounding edges or even beveling, a good wood *rasp* or a *plane* may come in handy.

As you build more and more lamps, you may discover other tools that make the process as simple and precise as you wish.

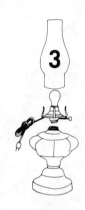

25 Lamps
Anyone Can Make

This chapter illustrates and gives basic instructions for making 25 lamps. Some of the lamps may strike you more than others (Fig. 3-1). Their purpose is to show you how easy lamps are to make. Study these diagrams and illustrations to learn the fundamentals of lamp making and then design your own lighting creations.

GUIDELINES TO FOLLOW

There are five lamp making rules to keep in mind. Follow them exactly or make your own set of guidelines to fill your lighting needs:

1. Generally, the distance between the bottom of a table lamp's shade and the floor is about 40 to 42 inches. If someone sits in a chair next to the lamp, the bottom of the shade should be at eye level.
2. If constructing a floor lamp, the finished product's shade should be about 47 inches from the floor.
3. If making a small bedside lamp, the distance between the bottom of the shade and the mattress of one's bed should be about 20 inches.
4. Any lamp that is constructed using a shade should be made so the glare of the light bulb does not show outside the shade.
5. All lamps you make should be heavy or stable enough so they are not easily tipped over.

Fig. 3-1. Examples of a few of the 25 lamps made from instructions given in Chapter 3.

Those are just a few rules of lamp making you may wish to consider. Most importantly the lamps you make should be appealing to yourself, and hopefully those around you.

IDEAS FOR LAMPS

The lamps that are constructed in this book came from many different sources. Below is a list giving the lamp's name and where the object was found or purchased to give you an idea how easy it is to find decorative and unique objects that can be turned into lamps.

Quick bottle lamp—a gallon vinegar jar purchased from a grocery store.

Whiskey bottle—originally purchased at a liquor store.

Interior lighted bottle lamp—this bottle was purchased at a rummage sale.

Candle holder lamp—purchased from a shop in Mexico.

Tin can lamp—smoking section of a drug store.

Wrought-iron mantel lamp—this was made by a friend when he was in school.

Metal lighthouse lamp—gift shop.

Milk can lamp—purchased from a small country store.

Child's lamp—cookie jar that was purchased in a department store.

Fire extinguisher—salvaged from an old building.

Hanging lampshade—any lamp store will have plenty of shades to choose from.

Hanging basket lamp—purchased at one of the chain department stores.

Two-basket lamp—both baskets were purchased from a chain department store.

Driftwood lamp—found in a wash.

Turned wood lamp—lumber supply store.

Wood and rope—lumber supply store.

Butcher block lamp—department store or housewares shop.

Ceramic monkey lamp—any gift shop should have similar ceramic pieces.

Vase lamp—gift shop.

Flower pot lamps—nursery or department store that sells potted plants.

Picture frame lamp—purchased from a photographic supply store but frame shops should carry similar frames.

Wall lamp—piece of oak salvaged from a table top that was to be thrown away.

Mannequin floor lamp—found in a trash can but can be purchased from stores that specialize in materials for display.

Wood and copper floor lamp—lumber supply and a plumbing supply store.

Oak table lamp—lumber supply, plumbing store and table top was salvaged from the trash. Some stores sell unfinished furniture that can be transformed into table lamps.

As you can see, lamp making materials can be found just about anywhere you look. It all depends on how you look at the object, and whether or not you are willing to transform the object into a lamp.

Quick Bottle Lamp

Fig. 3-2. Filling a gallon bottle with pinto beans makes an attractive base for this quick-to-make lamp.

There's really very little instruction needed in constructing this gallon bottle lamp.

A lamp adapter kit is purchased. The kit includes a socket that is already wired with an electrical cord and plug. Beneath the socket is a tapered adapter that fits several different-sized openings of bottles. The lamp's shade has a built-in butterfly harp that fits over the light bulb.

Simply, the socket adapter is slipped into the opening of the bottle. However, a plain looking gallon jar has little appeal by itself.

Fig. 3-3. A lamp adapter kit is pushed into the opening of the bottle and the lamp is almost finished.

To add aesthetic value the jar is filled with dry, pinto beans before inserting the adapter (Fig. 3-2).

The bottle could also be filled with sand, macaroni, sea shells, or anything else you might think of. The bottle contained vinegar before it was cleaned and transformed into a lamp.

Absolutely no tools are needed for this lamp's construction.

MATERIALS

Lamp adapter kit
Bottle
Fill material: beans, macaroni, sea shells, sand, rock, etc.
Desired shade

CONSTRUCTION STEPS

1. Fill bottle with decorative material.
2. Insert lamp adapter kit (Fig. 3-3). At times some lamp adapters do not fit as snugly as they should. This can be corrected by wrapping tape around the tapered adapter to increase its width so it will stay firmly in the bottle's opening.
3. Insert bulb into socket and attach lampshade.

Whiskey Bottle Lamp

Fig. 3-4. A small whiskey bottle lamp.

Fig. 3-5. A flattering shade needs to be chosen.

Here's a small 7-inch based lamp that works well as a decorative night light on top of your dresser. You may need to search to find a whiskey bottle similar to this one (Fig. 3-4).

A little more work is involved in making this lamp than the quick bottle lamp. A brass and cork lamp adapter is used. The most difficult task is drilling a hole through the base of the bottle with a masonry bit.

Once you have drilled a small ¼-inch hole, the electrical cord can be run through the bottle and then the adapter. The socket base is screwed into place on the nipple of the adapter and the electrical cord is stripped and attached to the terminals of the socket. Push the socket back together and add a plug and the lamp is almost finished.

Two shades are available for the finishing touch (Fig. 3-5). Both shades have a built-in harp that slips over the bulb. You can see how a lampshade changes the appearance of a lamp by comparing Fig. 3-4 and Fig. 3-6.

MATERIALS

Lamp adapter
Socket
Electrical wire and plug
Bulb and shade
Proper tools

58

Fig. 3-6. The shade can change a lamp's appearance.

Fig. 3-7. The basic materials used to make a whiskey bottle lamp.

CONSTRUCTION STEPS

1. Drill a ¼-inch hole through the base of the bottle with a masonry bit (Fig. 3-7).
2. Attach the base of the socket to the lamp adapter.
3. Run the electrical wire through the hole in the base of the bottle and through the lamp adapter and socket base.
4. Strip the insulation from the electrical wire and attach to the two socket terminals. Press the socket back together. Insert the adapter and light socket into the bottle's opening.
5. Attach a plug to the other end of the electrical wire.
6. Add a light bulb to the socket and attach an appropriate lampshade. .

Lighted Bottle Lamp

Fig. 3-8. A large interior-lighted bottle lamp.

Here's a slightly different approach to a lamp made from a bottle. This is an exceptionally large and heavy bottle purchased at a rummage sale. The dark amber color enables a set of small, orna-

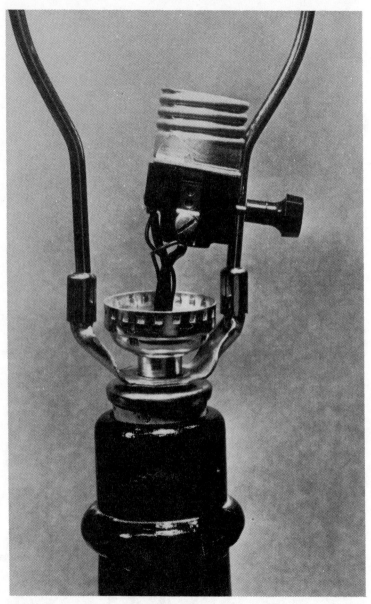

Fig. 3-9. The interior lights and electrical cord are both attached to the socket terminals.

Fig. 3-10. The dark color of the bottle makes the interior lights almost invisible except when the lights are on.

mental lights to be placed inside the bottle that become visible only when the lights are on (Fig. 3-8).

A tungsten-carbide drill is used to make a ¼-inch hole in the base of the bottle. A lamp adapter of cork and brass is used in the opening of the neck. Both the wires from the ornamental lights and the electrical cord are attached to the socket's terminals. A 12-inch removable harp is used in the construction of this lamp.

The current from the wall socket runs directly to the small interior lights. They are on anytime the lamp is plugged in. To prevent the lamp from having to be unplugged when not in use, a small in-line switch is added to the electrical cord. This way the interior lights could be turned on and off; just the lights in the lamp's interior could be turned on; or both the interior lights and the socket's light could be turned on at the same time.

MATERIALS

Large, dark bottle
Lamp adapter
Socket
Small, ornamental lights
Electrical cord and plug
Harp, proper shade, and finial
Glass drilling tools

Fig. 3-11. To control the interior lights an in-line switch is attached to the electrical cord.

CONSTRUCTION STEPS

1. Drill a ¼ to ⅜ inch hole through the base of the bottle using a tungsten-carbide drill bit.
2. Insert the small decorative lights into the bottle. Leave the plug end hanging from the bottle's neck.
3. Pass the electrical cord through the hole near the base and through the opening in the neck.
4. Remove the plug from the decorative lights, if necessary, and then pass the electrical cord and light wires through the lamp adapter.
5. Strip away the insulation from the wires and slip them through the harp and socket base. Attach the wires to the terminals of the light socket (Fig. 3-9).
6. Push the socket back together once the base has been screwed into place on the adapter. Then insert the adapter and socket into the opening of the bottle (Fig. 3-10).
7. Attach an in-line switch to the electrical cord near the bottle so it's easy to reach. Then attach the necessary plug to the remaining end of the electrical cord (Fig. 3-11).
8. Attach the harp to the harp base, insert a proper bulb and attach your lampshade and finial.

Candle Holder Lamp

Fig. 3-12. A candle holder converted into an electric light.

This particular lamp is nothing more than a candle holder purchased in Mexico. As a candle burning light it was used only at Christmas and other holidays. Once it was converted into an electrical lamp, it was used daily as a night light (Fig. 3-12).

A small nipple is added to the candle holder to quickly convert it into a lamp. Instead of an ordinary socket a candlestick type socket is used (Fig. 3-13). There was on on/off mechanism on the socket, so an in-line switch is added to the electrical cord.

Many different candle holders can be converted into bulb-burning lamps.

MATERIALS

Candlestick holder
Small nipple
Candlestick socket and cover
In-line switch
Hexnut
Electrical cord and plug
Bulb
Proper tools for construction

Fig. 3-13. A nipple and candlestick socket is attached to the base of the candle holder.

CONSTRUCTION STEPS

1. Drill a ⅜-inch hole through the base of the candle holder.
2. Insert the nipple in the ⅜-inch hole and put a hexnut on one side and the candle socket on the other.
3. Insert the electrical cord through the nipple and strip away the insulation. Attach the bare wires to the socket's terminals.
4. Attach electrical plug and in-line switch to the cord.
5. Attach and cut, if necessary, the plastic sheath for the candle socket.
6. Add light bulb.

Tin Can Lamp

Fig. 3-14. Two tin can lamps.

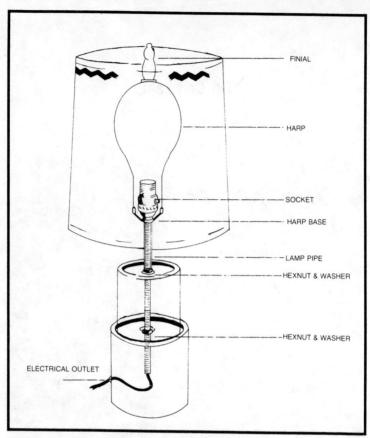

——— FINIAL

——— HARP

——— SOCKET

——— HARP BASE

——— LAMP PIPE

——— HEXNUT & WASHER

——— HEXNUT & WASHER

ELECTRICAL OUTLET

Fig. 3-15. Parts of the tin can lamp assembled.

These two lamps look like a great advertisement for Captain Black pipe tobacco. I happened to notice how these cans were stacked in the smoking section of a drug store. Fortunately the 7 and 14-ounce cans stack neatly. If you know any pipe smokers, you may want to see how their tobacco cans stack up to these (Fig. 3-14).

Thin metal is easily penetrated so holes were made in the top and bottom of the 7-ounce can. One hole is made in the top of the 14-ounce can. Totally threaded lamp pipe is cut to length, then inserted through the top and bottom of the smaller can. The lid is removed from the larger 14-ounce can and the lamp pipe inserted through it. Washers and hex-shaped nuts are used to hold the lamp pipe in place.

A ⅜-inch hole is drilled through the larger can near the bottom as an outlet for the electrical cord. Instead of a plastic or metal cord bushing inlet two hexnuts and a small piece of threaded lamp pipe is used.

The electrical cord passes through the larger can and then through the lamp pipe. A removable harp base is attached beneath the socket base.

I used sand in a plastic bag to give the lamp cans extra weight for stability. A wood base also could be used. A white shade was purchased and small black trim was glued to the top to help balance the black and white color. Figure 3-15 shows the parts of the completed lamp.

MATERIALS

Tin cans that stack neatly
Lamp pipe
Hexnuts and washers
Harp assembly, knob or finial
Socket
Bulb and proper shade
Electrical cord and plug
Base, if desired
Proper tools

Fig. 3-16. A washer and hexnut hold the lamp pipe in place on the top of the can.

Fig. 3-17. A hexnut and small nipple was used as an electrical cord outlet for the tin can lamp.

Fig. 3-18. The electrical cord passes through the lamp pipe.

CONSTRUCTION STEPS

1. Make a ⅜-inch hole in the top of both cans and the bottom of the smaller can. The holes should be in the center of each can.
2. Drill a ⅜-inch hole near the base of the larger can for an electrical cord inlet.
3. Insert the lamp pipe into the holes of the cans and secure in place with washers and hex or round nuts (Fig. 3-16).
4. Use a cord inlet bushing or use a small nipple and two hex-nuts to finish the cord hole at the base of the lamp (Fig. 3-17).
5. Run the electrical wire through the lamp, harp and socket base (Fig. 3-18).
6. Remove the insulation and attach the wires to the socket terminals.
7. Push the socket back into place and attach the harp and insert a light bulb.
8. Attach a plug to the electrical cord and add the shade and finial or knob of your choice.

Wrought-Iron Mantel Lamp

Fig. 3-19. A wrought-iron mantel lamp.

Here's a decorative object a friend of mine constructed while he was taking a metal working course in school. The wrought-iron work lends itself to a decorative lamp for over a mantel (Fig. 3-19).

Two well-placed holes are drilled for small ½-inch nipples. It's especially important in this lamp that the holes are drilled correctly to get them as straight as possible. One of the sockets leans a little, but it's not too noticeable when the shades are in place.

The most difficult aspect of constructing this lamp, other than making a wrought-iron figure yourself, is splicing together the electrical cord.

The insulation has to be scraped away from two of the wires without cutting them in two. A second wire, which runs to the plug, is then woven around the two bare wires (Fig. 3-20) and covered with electrical tape (Fig. 3-21) that has to blend well with the color of the cord. Fortunately the wire used here is black, and electrical tape also is black (Fig. 3-22).

It needs to be done in a place where the splice is least apt to show. In this case it's directly under the base of the wrought-iron figure. The splice should be done before the two opposite ends of the shorter cord are attached to the sockets.

Very small matching shades are used on candleflame-shaped bulbs. Candlestick sockets and their covers would work as well, if not better, for this particular mantel lamp.

MATERIALS

Wrought-iron object
Two normal or candlestick sockets
Two small ½-inch nipples
Electrical cord and plug
Hexnuts
Electrical tape
In-line switch, if using candlestick sockets and covers
Bulbs and shades
Proper tools

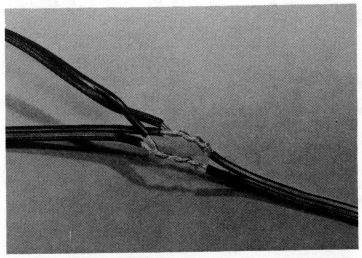

Fig. 3-20. Since two sockets are used a splice has to be made in the wire.

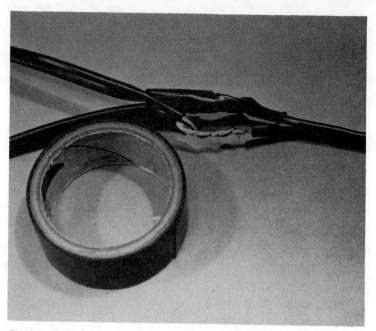

Fig. 3-21. Each splice has to be covered with electrical tape to prevent a short.

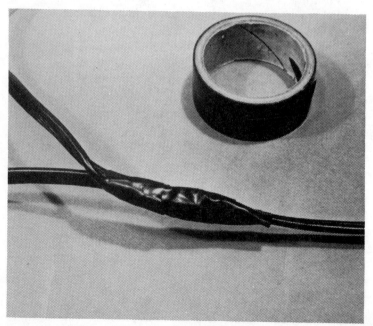

Fig. 3-22. Cover the splice completely with electrical tape.

Fig. 3-23. Poor drilling and the left side socket leans a little.

CONSTRUCTION STEPS

1. Drill ⅜-inch holes in the wrought-iron for nipples. Be sure the sockets won't lean (Fig. 3-23).
2. Attach the nipples with locknuts, or use a threading die for ⅛-I.P. nipples.
3. Splice the electrical cord to small piece of cord long enough to run from socket to socket. Cover the splice with electrical tape.
4. Pass the electrical cord through the nipples and base of sockets.
5. Strip away the insulation from both ends of the electrical cord and attach the copper wires to the socket terminals. When finished wiring push the sockets into place.
6. Attach a plug to remaining end of the electrical cord.
7. Attach in-line switch if candlestick sockets are used.
8. Add the bulbs and two identical shades.

Lighthouse Lamp

Fig. 3-24. A metal lighthouse converted into a night light.

This metal lighthouse was purchased at a gift shop. Originally the lighthouse had a music box inside that didn't work. So, what better object to turn into an attractive night light than a lighthouse (Fig. 3-24)?

A silver-colored socket, rather than the usual brass type, is used in construction. It blends much better with the black and metal appearance of the lighthouse (Fig. 3-25).

Fig. 3-25. A silver socket was used instead of brass to blend with the color of the lighthouse.

Fig. 3-26. Shade is too big; a smaller shade looks better.

A little prying is required to get the lighthouse apart. Next, holes are drilled through the lighthouse for the lamp pipe and outlet for the electrical cord. The lighthouse, being made of metal, is heavy enough by itself, therefore no base is needed.

The biggest problem with making the lamp is getting the lighthouse back together so it is again attached to its base. This is done by using small, unobtrusive metal screws that are later painted black.

This lamp is shown with two different shades (Fig. 3-26). The smaller of the two is more appealing, showing more of the lighthouse structure.

Fig. 3-27. The lamp pipe runs through the center of the lighthouse and is held in place by a hexnut and washer on one end and the socket's base on the other.

MATERIALS

Metal lighthouse
Silver-colored socket
Electrical cord and plug
Threaded lamp pipe
Washer and hex-shaped nut
Small metal screws
Small bulb and shade
Proper tools

CONSTRUCTION STEPS

1. Four ⅜-inch holes are drilled through the lighthouse after it's disassembled. Two are for the lamp pipe and two for an outlet for the electrical cord.
2. Lamp pipe is cut to the desired length and inserted through the center of the lamp and secured in place (Fig. 3-27). Only one washer and hexnut was used in the interior of the lamp. The base of the socket held the lamp pipe in place.
3. Electrical wire is passed through the two holes at the base and then through the lamp pipe and socket base. The

Fig. 3-28. Two holes were drilled for the cord outlet and a small metal screw holds the lighthouse in place.

82

insulation is removed from the wire and the wire is then attached to the socket's terminals.

4. The lighthouse is attached to the base (Fig. 3-28) with small metal screws, once the socket is secured in place. Small holes may need to be drilled to get the metal screws started.

5. A plug is attached to the electrical cord.

6. A small bulb is inserted in the socket and a shade with a built-in harp is put in place.

7. The metal screws can be painted with black paint to blend with the color of the lighthouse.

Milk Can Lamp

Fig. 3-29. Milk can table lamp.

Country stores in dairy country will have metal milk cans which can be converted into lamps (Fig. 3-29). A floor lamp can be made from large milk cans and table lamps from smaller ones (Fig. 3-30).

The heavy containers need a hole through the lid for the lamp pipe or nipple and a hole through the bottom or side for the electrical cord inlet. Secure the lamp pipe, wire the socket, add a shade and the lamp is done.

The milk can table lamp, illustrated here, is done a little differently. Instead of drilling a hole through the lid for the lamp pipe, a

Fig. 3-30. Milk cans come in different sizes.

brass ceiling or wall fixture cover is used. The brass cover is held in place using a piece of wood to fit the can's opening and small wood screws.

MATERIALS

Milk can
Brass electrical cord inlet
Socket
Harp assembly and finial
Small nipple 3 to 6 inches long
Washers and round or hex-shaped nuts
Electrical cord and plug
Brass cap if desired
Proper tools

Fig. 3-31. A brass cover and neck was used in the lamp's construction. It would be easier to just drill through the lid of the milk can.

CONSTRUCTION STEPS

1. Drill a ⅜-inch hole through the center of the milk can's lid and one near the bottom or base of the milk can (Fig. 3-31).
2. Insert the nipple through the hole in the lid and secure in place with washers and nuts.
3. Insert the brass cord inlet into hole at the bottom of the milk can and secure in place with a hexnut.
4. Attach the harp and socket base to the nipple.
5. Run the electrical cord through the inlet and nipple. Strip away the insulation and attach the wire to the socket terminals. Push socket into place.
6. Add the plug to the electrical cord.
7. Add the harp, bulb, proper shade and finial.

Child's Room Lamp

Fig. 3-32. Child's lamp made from a cookie jar.

If you have youngsters in the family, you may want to make them lamps of their own. You may even ask for their assistance during the lamp's construction. Here's an example of a lamp made from a metal and plastic cookie jar (Fig. 3-32). The lamp can be constructed in just a few minutes.

A metal and plastic cookie jar is selected as the material for the child's room because of its durability. It would be difficult for youngsters to damage the lamp.

Fig. 3-33. Lamp pipe is attached to the removable lid with washers and hexnuts.

Fig. 3-34. Run electrical wire through lamp base and up through lamp pipe and socket base.

MATERIALS

Cookie jar, this one is metal and plastic
Lamp pipe
Brass electrical cord inlet bushing
Washers, round and hex-shaped nuts
Electrical cord and plug
Harp assembly, if needed
Socket
Light bulb and lampshade
Tools for construction

CONSTRUCTION STEPS

1. Drill ⅜-inch holes through the center of the lid and near the base of the container for the lamp pipe and electrical cord outlet.
2. The brass electrical cord inlet is added to the lamp and locked in place with a hexnut.
3. The lamp pipe is inserted through the lid (Fig. 3-33). This particular piece of lamp pipe had to be threaded about an extra ½-inch. Secure in place with washers and nuts.
4. Socket base is added to the lamp pipe.
5. Electrical wire is run through the inlet and then up through the lamp pipe and socket base (Fig. 3-34). Insulation is removed and the bare wires are attached to the socket terminals.
6. Socket is pushed together. Electrical plug is then attached.
7. Light bulb and shade are added to the lamp.

Fire Extinguisher Lamp

Fig. 3-35. A copper and brass fire extinguisher.

Fig. 3-36. Cleaning and polishing the copper is the most difficult task.

This copper and brass fire extinguisher was once a common sight in many buildings. They've been replaced by red chemical extinguishers today. If you can find one of these beauties, they make an interesting table lamp (Fig. 3-35).

The biggest chore in making this lamp is cleaning or polishing the brass and copper. Three holes are drilled for lamp pipe and electrical cord after you make sure the extinguisher has been deactivated by a safety supply firm.

A small 6-inch nipple, brass vase cap or top, harp and socket are all there is to the lamp construction. A brass cord bushing inlet gives a finishing look.

The heavy weight of the metal extinguisher eliminates the need for a base. Finding an attractive shade that goes with the copper and brass color of the lamp may take some searching.

MATERIALS

Brass and copper fire extinguisher
6 to 8-inch nipple
Socket
Harp attachment
Turned brass top
Brass cord bushing inlet
Electrical cord and plug
Washers and hexnuts
Bulb, lampshade, and finial
Proper tools

Fig. 3-37. A brass top covers the nipple and any errors made in drilling through the fire extinguisher's lid.

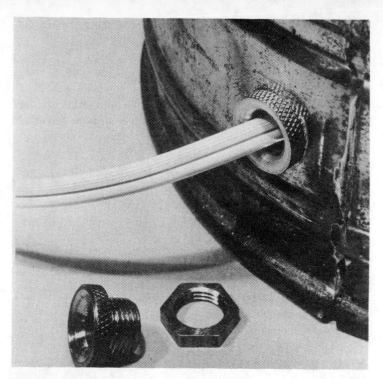

Fig. 3-38. A brass cord inlet helps give a finished look to the lamp.

CONSTRUCTION STEPS

1. Clean out the extinguisher by removing top after it has been deactivated by a local safety supply firm (Fig. 3-36).
2. Drill ⅜-inch holes through the center of the top, the bottom and out the backside near the base of the extinguisher.
3. Insert the nipple through the top and the decorative brass top and secure in place with washer and round or hex-shaped nuts (Fig. 3-37).
4. Insert the brass cord bushing inlet and lock in place with a hexnut.
5. Insert the electrical cord through the brass inlet (Fig. 3-38) and up through the extinguisher, nipple, harp and socket base. Screw extinguisher top in place.
6. Remove the insulation from the wire and attach to the terminals of the electric socket. Push the socket back into place.
7. Attach the plug to the electrical cord.
8. Insert bulb and attach lampshade and finial.

Hanging Lampshade Lamp

Fig. 3-39. A hanging lampshade lamp.

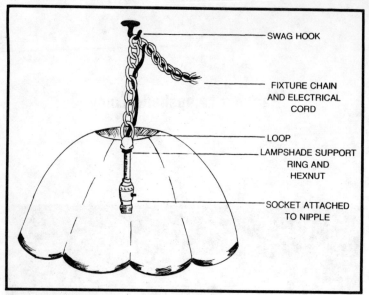

Fig. 3-40. Assembled parts of a hanging lamp.

Many large lampshades that have a center supporting ring can be converted into hanging lamps. Large, decorative shades make the most appealing hanging lamps for enhancing dark corners of the home (Fig. 3-39).

All that's needed is a socket without a switch, a nipple, loop and hexnut, and washer to hold everything in place (Fig. 3-40). The length of the nipple will depend on the size of the lamp shade being converted into a lamp. The nipple has to be long enough so the socket and light bulb will be near the center of the shade when the lamp is completed.

Fixture chain and a swag hook kit will be needed to hang the lamp. You'll want an extra long length of electrical cord and possibly an in-line switch.

MATERIALS

Decorative lampshade
Socket without switch
Proper length nipple or lamp pipe
Metal loop
Extra long length of electrical cord and plug
Fixture chain and swag hook kit
In-line on/off switch, if necessary
Proper tools

Fig. 3-41. Socket, nipple, hexnut, possibly a washer, loop, fixture chain and electrical cord is all that is needed to convert a lampshade into a hanging light fixture.

Fig. 3-42. The socket attaches to the center supporting ring of the lampshade. The fixture chain attaches to the loop with the electrical cord woven through the chain.

CONSTRUCTION STEPS

1. Attach the base of the socket to the end of the nipple or lamp pipe. Then attach the pipe to the lampshade by inserting through the support ring and securing in place using a washer and hexnut on the inside and the loop on the outside (Fig. 3-41).

2. Insert electrical cord through the loop's center and through the pipe and socket base.

3. Strip away the electrical cord's insulation and attach the bare copper to the terminals of the socket. Push the socket back together. Make sure that the socket is high enough in the shade, so when the bulb is added to the socket it is near the center or just below the shade's midpoint.

4. Attach the fixture chain to the loop and then weave the electrical cord through the chain (Fig. 3-42) and attach the plug.

5. If an on/off mechanism is needed, attach an in-line switch to the electrical cord where it can be easily reached when the shade is hanging.

6. Lamp is ready to hang using a swag hook kit.

Hanging Basket Lamp

Fig. 3-43. Some baskets can be converted into hanging light fixtures.

Fig. 3-44. A small brass cap or check ring adds decorative appeal and supports the loop on the outside of the basket.

Decorative baskets can enhance many home decors. Some can be easily converted into lamps, or even used as lampshades. Illustrated here is one basket that has been converted to a simple hanging light fixture that can brighten a dark corner (Fig. 3-43).

It's possible to make this light fixture without any tools except for a sharp knife to scrape away electrical cord insulation.

A small 4-inch nipple is passed through the center of the basket. No hole has to be made because there is one already centered on this particular basket.

A small brass cap and loop is used on the outside, and a washer and hexnut is used on the inside of the basket. An electrical socket without any switch was used. An in-line switch was later installed in the electrical cord.

Brass chain is attached to the loop and the electrical cord is weaved through the chain to make it as invisible as possible.

When using baskets for lamps, you want to make sure they are large enough so the bulb and socket are far enough away from the basket material to prevent prolonged use from heating the basket. Incandescent bulbs get very hot, and it's possible that contact with flammable basket material could cause a fire.

MATERIALS

Large, decorative basket
6 to 8-inch nipple
Switchless socket
Brass cap
Hexnut and washer
Fixture chain
Loop
In-line switch
Extra long length of electrical cord and plug
To hang—swag hook kit
Proper tools

CONSTRUCTION STEPS

1. If necessary make a hole through the center of the basket's base and insert nipple. Then secure the nipple in place with a hexnut and a washer on the inside of the basket and a brass loop and brass cap on the outside (Fig. 3-44).
2. Insert the electrical cord through the loop, nipple and socket base.
3. Strip the insulation from the electrical cord and attach the wires to the socket's terminals. Push the socket in place.
4. Attach the fixture chain to the loop and weave the electrical cord through the chain.
5. Hang the finished lamp from the swag hooks at the desired height. Cut the electrical cord to the proper length and attach the plug.
6. If the electrical outlet used for the hanging lamp is not controlled by a wall switch, insert an in-line switch in the cord at an accessible place.
7. Add light bulb.

Two-Basket Lamp

Fig. 3-45. Two identical baskets make an interesting table lamp.

Here's another variation of a lamp you can make from baskets. This time two baskets are used to construct a unique table lamp (Fig. 3-45). There are many variations possible using baskets. This is a simple one to construct.

Two identical, but rigid baskets are used. The open areas in the basket's weave produce interesting shadows when the lamp's bulb is on.

The construction of the baskets eliminates the need to drill or make holes for the lamp pipe. A small nipple is passed through the bottom of one basket and secured in place with a washer and hexnut on the inside. A coupling and washer is used on the exterior and covered with a brass cap. A 10-inch length of lamp pipe threaded on each end is passed through the brass cap and screwed into the coupling beneath the cap. A hexnut above the cap holds the lamp pipe and cap in place.

Fig. 3-46. A brass cap and hexnut help support the lamp pipe on the outside of the basket used for the lamp's base. A washer and hexnut are used on the inside of the basket. The cap also hides a small coupling.

A detachable harp base is attached to the lamp pipe and held in place by a hexnut and the socket's base. Electrical cord is inserted near the bottom of the basket (actually the top, if the basket were right side up) and passed through the nipple and lamp pipe.

The wire's insulation is removed and then attached to a socket. A plug is added to the electrical cord, and the harp is attached to its base.

The remaining basket is attached to the harp using a washer and finial. A bulb is added and you have a finished lamp.

MATERIALS

Two identical, sturdy baskets
Small 2 to 4-inch nipple
10 to 12-inch lamp pipe
Coupling
Brass cap or top
Washers and round or hex-shaped nuts
Socket
Electrical wire and plug
Harp assembly and finial
Bulb
Proper tools

CONSTRUCTION STEPS

1. Insert the nipple into the center of one basket and secure in place with a washer and hexnut on the inside of the basket and a coupling on the outside.
2. Pass the lamp pipe through brass cap or top after putting on round or hex-shaped nut. Then screw lamp pipe into the coupling. The lamp pipe should be secured (Fig. 3-46).
3. Run the electrical wire from the bottom of the basket through the weave. If necessary, make a hole for the electrical cord. Pass the wire through the nipple and lamp pipe.
4. Attach a hexnut and then harp and socket base to the top of the lamp pipe. Strip the insulation from the electrical cord and attach to the terminals of the socket. Push socket in place.
5. Attach the plug to the other end of the electrical cord.
6. Add the harp and screw a light bulb into the socket. Then rest the remaining basket on top of the harp and secure in place with a finial and washers, if necessary.

Driftwood Lamp

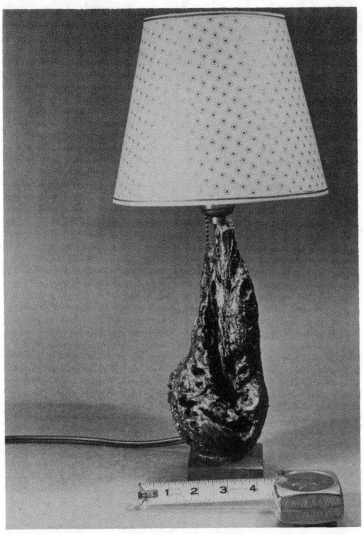

Fig. 3-47. A small piece of driftwood converted into a lamp.

Fig. 3-48. The small wooden base was attached to the driftwood with a wood screw that was countersunk.

Weathered woods of different sizes can be converted into attractive lamps, depending on the appeal of the wood's shape and color. Even wood that is painted, as the one illustrated here, can be unique and decorative (Fig. 3-47).

Seldom will you find a piece of driftwood that will sit flat by itself. Care has to be taken to either sand or saw one edge of the wood so the finished lamp will sit correctly, whether it's on a base or standing alone.

Some wood pieces will have natural cavities to hide electrical cord. If not, holes will have to be drilled to hold the cord and the lamp pipe.

If the wood is to be painted, commercial wood fillers can be used to hold the lamp pipe in place and give a finished look. If the wood is to be left natural, care must be taken in drilling and fitting pieces so the lamp parts and wood blend together.

MATERIALS

Socket
Drift or weathered wood
Electrical cord and plug
Wood filler, if needed
Base, if needed
Harp, if needed
Hexnuts, and washers
Wood screws, if needed
Bulb and shade
Proper tools for construction

Fig. 3-49. The lamp was to be painted so wood filler material was used to help hold the lamp pipe in place.

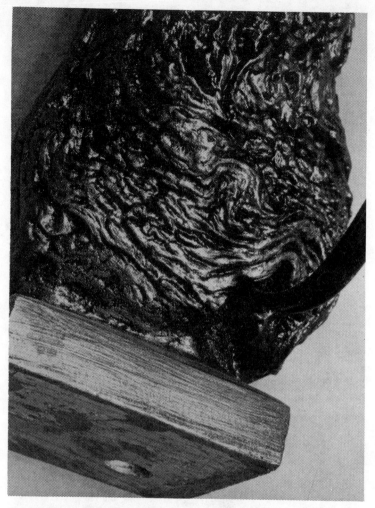

Fig. 3-50. The electrical cord passed out a natural opening in the wood.

CONSTRUCTION STEPS

1. Once you have found an attractive piece of wood, find out which way it sits best. Using a saw, cut as straight a cut as you can so the material will sit flat on either a lamp base or other flat surface.
2. Drill the appropriate hole through the wood for the lamp pipe and electrical cord outlet. If a lamp base is needed you may have to countersink a hole in the bottom for a washer and hexnut. If the base is used only as a support it can be

attached to the wood using wood screws that have been countersunk (Fig. 3-48).

3. Insert the lamp pipe in the ⅜-inch hole you have drilled. If the wood is to be painted, filler material can be used around the lamp pipe to hold it in place (Fig. 3-49). If the wood is not to be painted, you will have to run the lamp pipe all the way through the wood. It can run through the base, if needed, or it can be attached to the bottom of the wood being converted into a lamp with a hexnut that has been countersunk.

4. Run the electrical cord through the lamp pipe, harp, and socket base (Fig. 3-50). Strip away the insulation and attach the bare wires to the socket terminals. The electrical cord outlet can either be at the back side of the wood being turned into a lamp or it can run through the backside of the lamp's base.

5. Large decorative driftwood lamps may need a detachable harp. Small lamps will not need a harp because it will come with the shade.

6. Attach the socket and then attach the plug to the other end of the electrical cord.

7. Leave the wood natural, paint, or seal with stain, varnish or other wood finishing material.

8. Add the bulb and shade.

Turned Wood Lamp

Fig. 3-51. A piece of turned wood from a lumber supply store is easily turned into a lamp.

Many lumber supply stores have pieces of turned wood that can be converted into decorative lamps. The lamp shown here is made from a 12-inch piece of wood that was cut down to 10 inches (Fig. 3-51).

The most difficult aspect of this lamp's construction is drilling a hole through the wood's center. A bit extension is needed to drill through the long length of wood. Bit extensions require the use of a ⅝-inch bit or larger. If a ⅝-inch bit is used, the hole will be ¼-inch larger than actually needed. But that is all right.

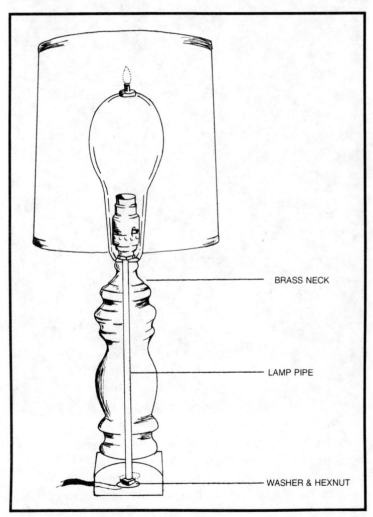

Fig. 3-52. Parts of a turned wood lamp.

Fig. 3-53. The wood was cut to have more appeal as a lamp.

The extra 2/8-inch allows for error in your drilling. It's very difficult to drill a straight 10-inch hole. With the extra 2/8ths, you can move the lamp pipe around the hole until it's straight.

This type of lamp lends itself to pairs. You may decide to make two identical lamps for your home. Figure 3-52 shows the parts of a turned wood lamp after assembly.

MATERIALS

Turned wood column
Brass top or cap
Lamp pipe
Socket
Harp assembly
Washers and nuts
Electrical cord and plug
Light bulb and lampshade
Tools for construction

Fig. 3-54. The wood that was cut from the column might be used as a lamp base.

CONSTRUCTION STEPS

1. The turned wood column may have to be cut with a saw to remove one end (Fig. 3-53). Do so if necessary. The wood that was cut from the column might be used as a lamp base (Fig. 3-54).
2. Sand or file the wood column's top until the brass cap fits (Fig. 3-55).
3. Drill a ⅝-inch hole (using a bit extension) through the length of the column after drilling a 1-inch countersink hole in the column's base (Fig. 3-56).

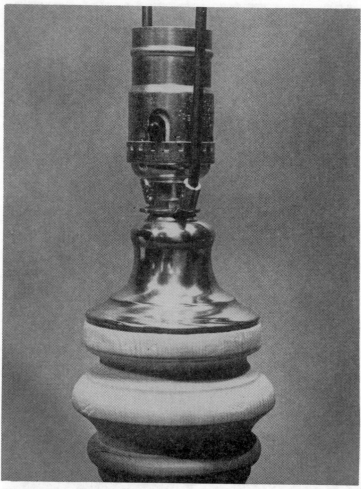

Fig. 3-55. The wood was sanded to fit the size of the brass top.

Fig. 3-56. A 1-inch bit was used to countersink a hole for the lamp pipe, washer, hexnut, and electrical cord.

4. Drill a ¼-inch hole through the back of the wood column for an electrical cord outlet. The ½-inch hole should come out somewhere in the area of the 1-inch countersunk hole in the column's base.
5. Insert lamp pipe through the column and brass top. Secure in place with washers and nuts.
6. Attach harp and socket base to the lamp pipe.
7. Sand and paint or stain the wood column. Allow to dry.
8. Strip away the electrical cord's insulation and attach the bare wires to the socket terminals. Push socket into place.
9. Add the electrical plug.
10. Add harp, socket, shade and finial.

Wood and Rope Lamp

Fig. 3-57. Wood and manila rope make an interesting lamp.

Fig. 3-58. Once the wood is cut and a tin can wrapped with rope, the lamp can be quickly made.

Fig. 3-59. The rope is inserted into holes in the can and held in place by tying a knot or inserting a small nail through the rope.

Fig. 3-60. A countersunk hole allows for a washer, hexnut and an outlet hole for the electrical cord.

Here's a rustic looking lamp that you can make from start to finish. With a little imagination it can be modified in appearance and size (Fig. 3-57).

You'll have to use some woodworking tools—saw, plane, file—and do some sanding to finish the project. The lamp is nothing more than an empty tin can wrapped with manila rope and centered between two pieces of wood.

Any wood will work—pine, mahogany, oak, birch—or anything you might have handy. Dimensions will depend on the size of the can you use. It can be a quart or a rectangular gallon can.

This is one lamp that requires a base of fairly thick dimensions so the electrical cord can run out the backside. A hole will have to be countersunk for the hexnut and washer supporting the lamp pipe.

MATERIALS

Wood
Sandpaper, paint or stain for finishing wood
Lamp pipe
Hexnuts and washers
Tin can
Socket
Manila rope
Harp assembly and finial, if needed
Brass top, if needed
Electrical cord and plug
Bulb and desired shade
Proper tools

Fig. 3-61. Once the lamp's base is made and stained or painted, add a brass neck and the electrical plug.

Fig. 3-62. A harp attached to the top of the socket was used on this lamp.

CONSTRUCTION STEPS

1. Cut the top and base for the lamp. (The one illustrated is 5 by 7 inches.) Two pieces of wood were joined for the base. Either round or plane the edges of the wood (Fig. 3-58).

2. Take an empty tin can and cut the remaining end away with a can opener. Make two large holes at the edge of each end. Insert the rope in one of the holes and tie in a knot. Then wrap the can with the rope as tightly as possible. Inset the rope in the remaining hole and tie a knot or slide a small nail through the rope so it remains in place. Make sure none of the can's metal shows (Fig. 3-59).

3. Drill a ⅜-inch hole in the center of the top piece of wood you made for the lamp. For the base you need to drill a 1-inch hole halfway through the center of the wood. Then drill the rest of the way with a ⅜-inch bit. Next, drill a ¼-inch hole from the back of the base low enough so it comes out in the area of the 1-inch hole. This will be an outlet for the lamp's electrical cord (Fig. 3-60).

4. Sand and then paint or stain the two pieces of wood. Let dry.

5. Cut or buy the proper length lamp pipe. Insert the lamp pipe through the base and through the center of the tin can and the top piece of wood. Use a washer and hexnut in the 1-inch hole and a hexnut and washer on the top of the lamp. This will hold the lamp together (Fig. 3-61).

6. Insert the electrical cord through the hole on the backside of the base and then up through the lamp pipe. Add a decorative brass top, if desired, and then the base of the socket and harp base, if needed (Fig. 3-62).

7. Strip away the insulation from the electrical cord and attach to the socket's terminals. Push socket in place.

8. Add a plug to remaining end of the electrical cord.

9. Add a light bulb and lampshade.

Butcher Block Lamp

Fig. 3-63. A butcher block lamp.

Colorful wood makes an interesting table lamp. Butcher block has always been an attractive wood whether it's been oiled or not. Large butcher blocks can be cut down to make attractive lamps (Fig. 3-63).

This butcher block is used just the way it was purchased from the store. It's 12 inches tall and 8-½ inches wide. Instead of using a base on the lamp, a small but heavy piece of wood is used as a support on the back side.

The one-inch width of the butcher block prevents drilling all the way through the wood. There would be too much chance for drilling error. So instead of taking a chance and damaging the wood, a cord inlet hole is drilled from the back side of the block. Figure 3-64 shows the back view.

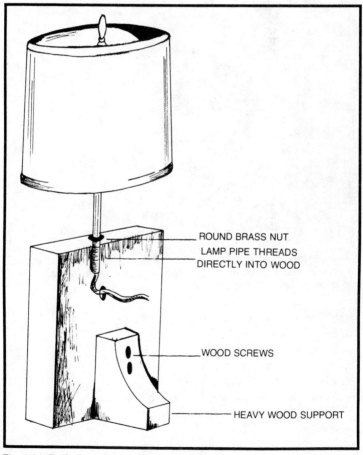

ROUND BRASS NUT
LAMP PIPE THREADS
DIRECTLY INTO WOOD

WOOD SCREWS

HEAVY WOOD SUPPORT

Fig. 3-64. Back view of a butcher block lamp.

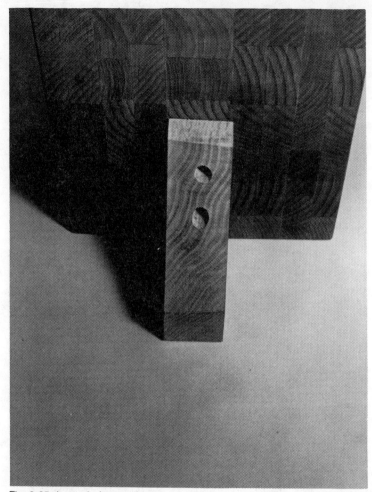

Fig. 3-65. Instead of a wood base a support was attached to the back of the butcher block using wood screws.

MATERIALS

Butcher block
Lamp pipe
Round retaining nut
Electrical cord and plug
Wood block or blocks for butcher block support
Small wood screws
Socket
Light bulb and lampshade
Proper tools for construction

CONSTRUCTION STEPS

1. Drill a hole in the center of the top part of the butcher block. The bit should be smaller than the ⅜-inch normally used. That way you can thread the lamp pipe directly into the wood. Drill as deep as you can go and drill as straight as possible.
2. Drill a hole on the back side of the butcher block so you hit (drill into) the hole you drilled from the top.
3. Cut one or two pieces of heavy wood to support the butcher block. Attach the pieces of wood with wood screws that have been countersunk (Fig. 3-65).
4. Screw in the lamp pipe after attaching a round nut.
5. Insert the electrical cord through the lamp pipe top and out the electrical cord outlet you have made.
6. Strip away the insulation from the electrical cord and attach the bare wires to the socket terminals after the socket base has been attached. Push the socket in place.
7. Add an electrical plug.
8. Add the light bulb and a flattering shade.

Ceramic Monkey Lamp

Fig. 3-66. Ceramic pieces are easy to convert into lamps.

Decorative items of ceramic come in all shapes and sizes. This little monkey is converted into a lamp for a child's room (Fig. 3-66).

Ceramic items are generally hollow so once holes are drilled for the lamp pipe and electrical cord outlet, the lamp can be quickly made.

If holes are drilled correctly, you may not need a brass cap as illustrated here. An error was made in drilling and it had to be covered up. When constructing lamps and errors are made, don't give up on the project until you're sure there is no way to cover up or correct the mistake.

MATERIALS

Ceraminc work
Nipple
Socket
Washers and hexnuts
Small brass cap if drilling mistake is made
Electrical cord and plug
Proper tools

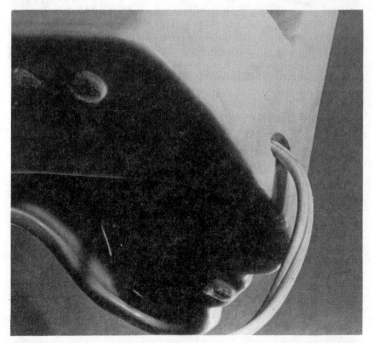

Fig. 3-67. A small hole is drilled out the back of the ceramic piece for the electrical cord.

Fig. 3-68. The brass check ring was used to cover up a drilling mistake.

CONSTRUCTION STEPS

1. Drill a ⅜-inch hole at top of ceramic work using a masonry bit.
2. Drill a ¼-inch hole near the base of the ceramic object for the electrical cord outlet (Fig. 3-67).
3. Attach a washer and hexnut on one end of the small nipple. Insert through the hole at the top of the ceramic work from inside.
4. Add brass cap if necessary to nipple. Attach hexnut or socket base to nipple (Fig. 3-68).
5. Run the electrical cord through the inlet at the base and then through the nipple and socket base. Strip away the insulation and attach the wires to the socket terminals. Push the socket into place.
6. Add the electrical plug.
7. Add the light bulb and lampshade with a built-in harp.

Vase Lamp

Fig. 3-69. Vases of all sizes can be converted into lamps.

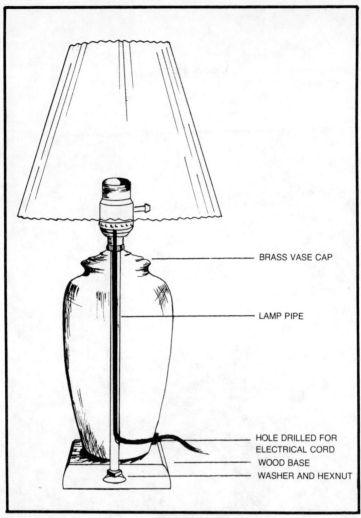

BRASS VASE CAP

LAMP PIPE

HOLE DRILLED FOR
ELECTRICAL CORD
WOOD BASE
WASHER AND HEXNUT

Fig. 3-70. Parts of a vase lamp.

Vases come in all shapes and sizes. Most can be converted into lamps. A base is needed to support the lamp pipe and hold the lamp together (Fig. 3-69).

Once a properly fitted brass vase cap or top is found and a hole is drilled through the bottom or side of the vase, the lamp can be quickly constructed.

If additional weight other than the base is needed for lamp stability, sand in plastic bags can be tucked inside the base. Figure 3-70 shows the parts of a vase lamp.

Fig. 3-71. Some vases will need a base to give needed stability to the finished lamp.

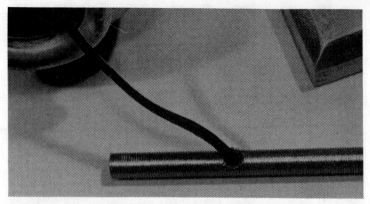

Fig. 3-72. The lamp pipe ran through the base and top of the vase. The electrical cord passed out a hole near the bottom of the vase. It was necessary to drill a small hole in the lamp pipe to allow for the electrical cord to pass out the back side of the lamp instead of out the back side of the wood lamp base.

MATERIALS

Decorative vase
Base material, if needed
Brass vase cap
Lamp pipe
Socket
Washers and hexnut
Electrical cord and plug
Light bulb and lampshade
Tools for construction

CONSTRUCTION STEPS

1. Make or purchase a base for the vase, if needed. A small decorative base was used for the vase here (Fig. 3-71).
2. Drill a ⅜-inch hole through the bottom of the vase if a base is used. If the electrical cord is to pass through the back of the lamp, as illustrated, drill a small ¼-inch hole for the electrical cord outlet. Drill a 1-inch countersinking hole through the bottom of the base and then finish the hole with a ⅜-inch bit.
3. The lamp pipe runs through the vase and then through the base and holds the lamp together. To allow for the electrical cord to pass through the lamp pipe, a small ¼-inch hole was drilled through one side of the lamp pipe (Fig. 3-72).
4. Sand, stain or paint the lamp base, if needed. Let dry.

Fig. 3-73. A brass electrical cord inlet was used to give a finished look to the vase lamp.

5. Insert the electrical cord through the hole drilled near the lamp's base (Fig. 3-73) and then through the hole in the lamp pipe and out one end.

6. Insert the lamp pipe in the base and through the hole in the bottom. Secure in place with a hexnut, and washer at the bottom of the base.

7. Slide vase cap over lamp pipe and fasten in place with nut or use the socket's base.

8. Strip away the electrical cord's insulation and attach the bare wires to the socket terminals. Push socket in place.

9. Add electrical plug.

10. Add bulb and decorative shade.

Flower Pot Lamps

Fig. 3-74. Clay flower pots can be turned into table lamps.

A common clay flower pot can be transformed into a decorative lamp. The pots can be used right side up, or upside down. You can decide for yourself which is more appealing (Fig. 3-74).

These 8-inch flower pots are quickly converted into lamps once the holes are drilled with a masonry bit for the electrical cord outlet.

One lamp makes use of the drainage hole as an opening for the lamp pipe. A brass cap is added for decorative appeal.

The right side up clay pot lamp requires a wood support for the lamp pipe. The support needs to be heavy (two-inch oak was used for this lamp) and fit snugly inside the flower pot. A few artificial, but decorative plants hide the support when the lamp is finished.

If you have found your thumb is no longer green, you may want to make use of your flower pots and convert one or two into lamps.

Fig. 3-75. A brass cap and lamp pipe used the drainage hole in the bottom of the clay pot.

Fig. 3-76. A check ring or washer is used in the inside of the pot to hold the lamp pipe in place. Two round nuts and a small nipple were used as the electrical cord inlet.

MATERIALS

Clay pot
Electrical cord inlet or small nipple and two round nuts
Large brass cap
Lamp pipe
Socket
Electrical cord and plug
Washer and round or hex-shaped nuts
Proper tools

CONSTRUCTION STEPS

1. Drill a ⅜-inch hole for the electrical cord outlet near the top of the flower pot using a masonry bit.
2. Insert the electrical cord bushing or nipple and two round nuts.
3. Insert the lamp pipe through the brass cap and drainage hole of the flower pot. Secure in place with washer and hexnuts (Fig. 3-75).
4. Attach socket base to lamp pipe and run the electrical cord through the inlet and lamp pipe (Fig. 3-76).
5. Strip away the insulation and attach the bare wires to the socket's termnals. Push socket into place.
6. Add the electrical plug.
7. Add bulb and desired lampshade.

RIGHT SIDE UP FLOWER POT LAMP MATERIALS

Clay flower pot
Wood for lamp pipe support
Lamp pipe
Socket
Washers and hexnuts
Electrical cord inlet, if desired
Electrical cord and plug
Bulb and lampshade
Selection of artificial plants
Modeling clay
Tools for construction

Fig. 3-77. The wood support should fit snugly inside the clay pot.

CONSTRUCTION STEPS

1. Drill a ⅜-inch hole for the electrical cord through the base of the clay pot with a masonry bit.
2. Cut the piece of wood so it fits snugly in the pot, but does not touch the bottom of the pot or block the electrical cord outlet (Fig. 3-77).
3. Countersink a 1-inch hole, then drill the rest of the way with a ⅜-inch hole for the lamp pipe through the wood base you have made (Fig. 3-78).
4. Secure the lamp pipe to the wood base using washers and hexnuts.
5. Attach socket base to the lamp pipe. Then run the electrical cord through the inlet and up through the lamp pipe and socket base.
6. Strip away the cord's insulation and attach the bare wires to the socket's terminals. Push socket in place.

Fig. 3-78. A heavy piece of wood, a countersunk lamp pipe are all that's needed for a lamp pipe support.

Fig. 3-79. Some decorative artificial flowers around the pot hide the block of wood supporting the lamp pipe and socket. Children's modeling clay will help hold the lamp pipe base and artificial flowers in place.

7. Place wood base and lamp assembly into flower pot. Modeling clay placed around the wood will hold the base in place.
8. Add artificial foliage around lamp pipe. Make sure it is low enough to be below the socket (Fig. 3-79).
9. Add the electrical plug.
10. Add light bulb and lampshade.

Picture Frame Lamp

Fig. 3-80. A plastic picture frame can be turned into an interesting lamp that spotlights your favorite photograph.

Many homes have their walls covered with picture frames and photographs. Some picture frames can be converted into unusual lamps. What better way to spotlight your favorite photograph than under the light of a lamp? (Fig. 3-80).

Illustrated here is an 8 by 10-inch plastic box frame that was converted into a lamp by drilling two holes and adding a stability-giving wood base. The base is made from a piece of wood and painted black to match the photograph.

If you are one of those people who collect pictures and frames, you may want to try making a picture frame lamp to display your favorite photos. Keep in mind that vertical pictures give more height than horizontal (Fig. 3-81). If you don't have 8 × 10 pictures or larger, you can group small pictures to fill large frames.

MATERIALS

8 by 10-inch plastic picture frame
Wood base materials
Socket
Washers and hexnuts
Brass neck and check rings
Electrical cord inlet bushing

Lamp pipe
Electrical cord and plug
Suitable photograph for
    framing
Light bulb and lampshade
Proper tools

Fig. 3-81. Vertical pictures give the height needed for a table lamp.

CONSTRUCTION STEPS

1. Make a wood base for the plastic frame. The one illustrated here is about 9 inches long and 3 inches wide. The base should be heavy enough to support the finished lamp.
2. Drill a ⅜-inch hole through the top and bottom of the plastic frame.
3. Drill a 1-inch countersinking hole through the center of the base and finish the hole with a ⅜-inch bit.
4. You can either run the lamp pipe through the whole length of the frame or you can use two proper-sized nipples. One nipple will support the light socket and the other will hold the base to the frame (Fig. 3-82).

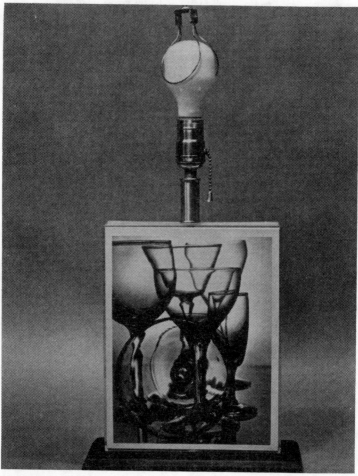

Fig. 3-82. Lamp pipe and socket attached to frame and base.

Fig. 3-83. A plastic cord inlet is used through the cardboard backing.

5. If a cardboard back is used to hold the picture in the frame, you may find it difficult to attach the washers and nuts to the nipples or lamp pipe. To make threading the nipples or lamp pipe easier you can cut a large hole in the cardboard backing. Secure nipples in place with washers and hexnuts.

6. Slip the neck over the lamp pipe with the check rings and fasten in place with hexnuts and socket base.

7. Once you are sure of putting the lamp together without having to make any more holes, you can take the lamp apart and put the picture in place. There should be no chance for damage now.

8. Sand and stain or paint the base you have constructed for the lamp. Let dry.

9. The electrical cord runs out the back of the frame or it can run out the back of the wood base you have constructed. If the cord runs out the back of the frame (Fig. 3-83), you may want to make a small hole and insert an electrical cord outlet.

10. Put the lamp back together after the base is dry and run the electrical cord through the lamp pipe and socket base. Strip away the insulation and attach to the socket's terminals. Push socket back together.

11. Add an electrical plug to the cord.

12. Add a light bulb and desired lampshade.

Wall Lamp

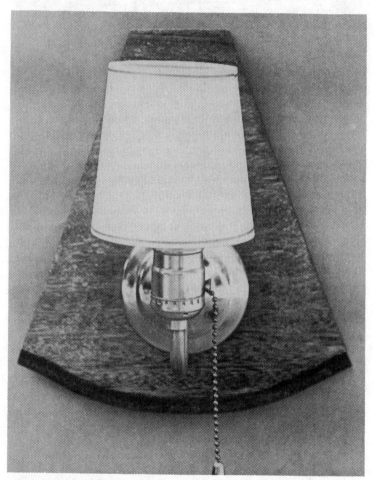

Fig. 3-84. Flat objects can be quickly turned into wall lamps.

The small wall lamp illustrated here is a remnant from an oak table that was headed for the garbage dump. A little sawing, sanding, and staining returned the wood to an attractive appearance.

After drilling one hole and adding a nipple, coupler, brass top and a piece of already-bent lamp pipe, I have the makings of a small wall lamp (Fig. 3-84).

Many flat, but decorative, objects can be converted into wall lamps. Metal, painted trays and dishes are examples. The bent lamp pipe makes for easy lamp conversion.

To install a wall lamp you may need a cross bar or bracket bar to attach the lamp to the wall. The bar has a threaded hole in the center for the nipple and two slots or holes for two screws. The assembly holds the wall lamp in place.

MATERIALS

Small decorative piece of wood
Bent lamp pipe
Nipple
Coupler
Brass top or cap
Washers and hexnuts
Socket
Short length of electrical cord
Bulb and shade
Tools for construction

Fig. 3-85. This small piece of oak was converted into a lamp using already-bent lamp pipe.

Fig. 3-86. All that's needed is a bulb, shade and a wall outlet for mounting.

CONSTRUCTION STEPS

1. Cut, sand and finish small piece of wood (Fig. 3-85).
2. Drill a ⅜-inch hole for the lamp pipe through the wood.
3. Insert nipple through hole and secure in place with a washer and hexnut on the backside of the wood and a coupler on the front side.
4. Put the brass cap over the coupling and secure in place with the bent piece of lamp pipe and a round or hex-shaped nut.
5. Attach socket base to the lamp pipe and run the electrical cord through the lamp pipe and socket base. Strip away the insulation and attach the bare wires to the socket's terminals.
6. Strip away insulation from electrical cord and add a cross bar to the nipple on the back side of the wall lamp.
7. Wall lamp is ready to be attached to wall outlet (Fig. 3-86).
8. Add light bulb and lampshade.

Mannequin Floor Lamp

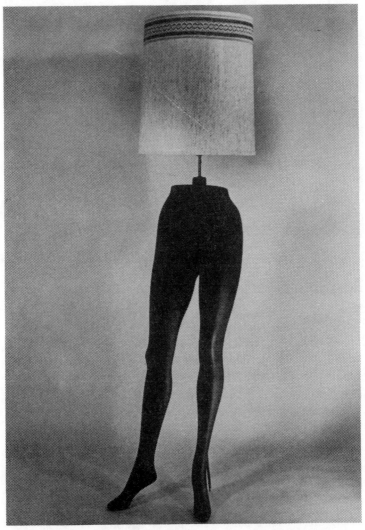

Fig. 3-87. The lower half of a mannequin makes an unusual floor lamp.

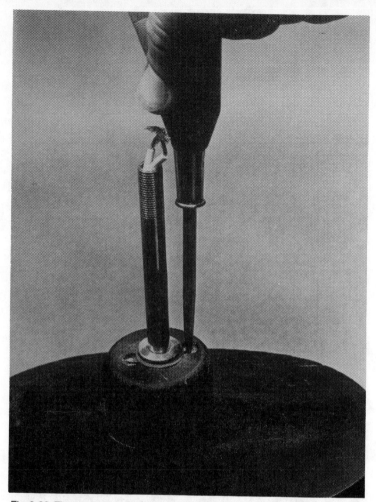

Fig. 3-88. The lamp pipe is inserted into the wood knob on top of the mannequin. The knob and lamp pipe are then screwed back into place.

A mannequin floor lamp is sure to draw comments from anyone who sees your lamp for the first time. This particular half of a mannequin was salvaged from the trash. A little plaster-of-paris to fill chipped areas and some flat black paint readies the mannequin for work—not as a clothes display, but as an unusual floor lamp.

Surprisingly, the mannequin legs are easily converted into a lamp (Fig. 3-87). The difficult part is running an electrical cord through one of the legs to the light socket. With the help of a straightened clothes hanger and piece of string, that is also accomplished.

If the mannequin doesn't have its own stand, a piece of pipe will work as a support.

As I constructed this particular lamp, I envisioned a large curving white lampshade and a well-placed red garter. I'm still looking for the red garter.

MATERIALS

Lower half of a mannequin
Lamp pipe
Harp assembly and finial
Washers and round or hex-shaped nuts
Electrical cord and plug
Bulb and shade
Proper tools

Fig. 3-89. Knob and lamp pipe in place.

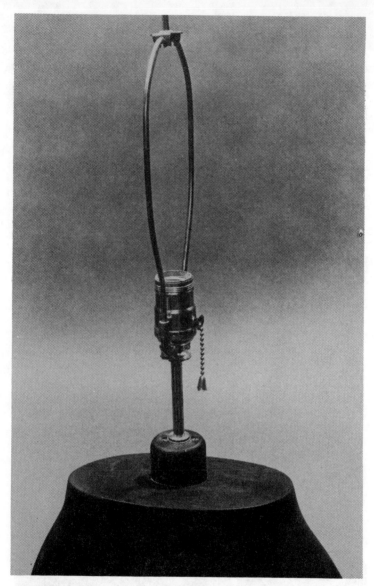

Fig. 3-90. A detachable harp assembly was used in the mannequin lamp's construction.

CONSTRUCTION STEPS

1. If necessary, repair and paint the mannequin.
2. Remove the wood knob from the top of the mannequin with a screwdriver.

3. The knob may have to be cut so that it is perpendicular to the ground.
4. Drill a 3/5-inch hole part way through the bottom side of the knob. Then drill the rest of the way with a ⅜-inch bit.
5. Drill a ⅜-inch hole through the top of the mannequin for the electrical cord and one through a foot for an electrical cord outlet.

Fig. 3-91. Socket pushed into place.

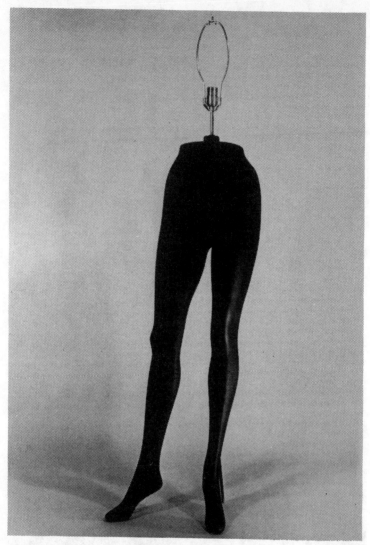

Fig. 3-92. Ready for an appropriate shade and finial.

6. Using a straightened clothes hanger, pass it through the mannequin. Tie a string to one end of the hanger and pull through the mannequin. Then tie or tape the electrical cord to the end of the string. Pull the electrical cord through the mannequin.
7. Attach the lamp pipe to the removed knob using nuts and washers (Fig. 3-88).

8. Pass the electrical cord through the lamp pipe. Then screw the knob and lamp pipe in place on top of the mannequin (Fig. 3-89).
9. Attach hexnut, harp and socket base to the end of the lamp pipe (Fig. 3-90).
10. Strip away the insulation from the lamp cord and attach the bare wires to the socket terminals. Push the socket into place (Fig. 3-91).
11. Add the plug to the electrical cord.
12. Add light bulb, harp and lampshade (Fig. 3-92).

Wood and Copper Floor Lamp

Fig. 3-93. Turned wood and copper make an attractive floor lamp.

Decorative floor lamps can be useful and supply light where there isn't any table or dresser to set a table lamp. The troublesome part of making a floor lamp is finding a base that you can run a long length of electrical cord through without having to drill a long, straight hole.

The problem is reduced with the lamp illustrated here (Fig. 3-93). You still have to drill a hole, but it's not 47 inches long. If a ¾-inch bit is used with a bit extension, you don't have to worry about how straight your hole is. It should be near the center, but the extra large hole allows for some drilling error.

Many floor lamps use lengths of brass tubing that have a ½ to 1-inch diameter. Instead of brass this lamp uses copper tubing that has an inside diameter of 1-inch. The copper discolors quickly as does bare brass.

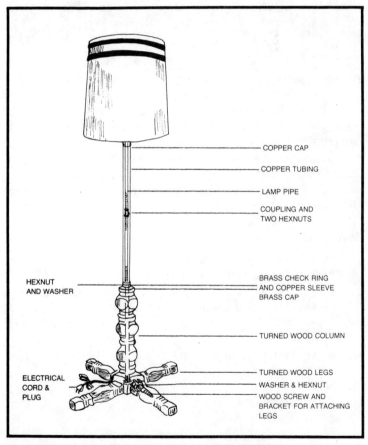

Fig. 3-94. Parts of wood and copper floor lamp assembled.

155

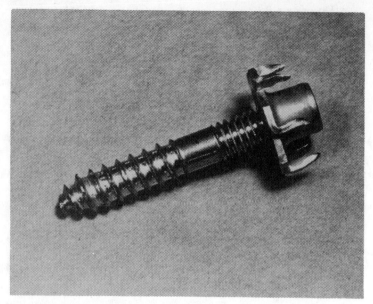

Fig. 3-95. Wood screws and metal bracket for attaching legs to column.

The wood base of the lamp is constructed from ready turned wood purchased from a lumber supply store. Four pieces of the base are actually table legs.

The wood base can be modified, depending on what type of turned wood you use. Keep in mind the four supporting legs should be similar in appearance to the column they are attached to. Figure 3-94 shows the parts of a floor lamp put together.

MATERIALS

24-inch turned wood column
Four 12-inch turned wood table legs
Copper tubing 26 inches long and with a 1-inch inside diameter
Copper sleeve and copper cap to fit tubing
Brass cap with a diameter equal to the top of the turned wood column
Brass check rings to fit copper tubing and sleeve, about 1-½ inch diameter
Socket
Harp assembly and finial
Electrical cord and plug
Washers and round or hex-shaped nuts
Proper tools and finishing materials

Fig. 3-96. Turned wood legs were attached using glue and special wood screws.

Fig. 3-97. A coupler is used to attach the lamp pipe together.

Fig. 3-98. A brass cap and check ring are used as decorative touches to the lamp.

CONSTRUCTION STEPS

1. Cut the turned wood columns, if necessary, to fit brass cap. 3-½ inches were removed from the turned wood column illustrated here.
2. Drill a ¾-inch hole through the column center after drilling a 1-inch counter sink hole in base.
3. Add the supporting legs by using the wood screws and brackets that generally are attached to the legs (Fig. 3-95). Screws may have to be reversed. Use glue for extra strength (Fig. 3-96). Let glue dry.

4. Insert desired length lamp pipe through column. 46-½ inch lamp pipe was used on this lamp. A coupling was used to get proper length (Fig. 3-97).
5. Washer and hexnut hold the bottom of lamp pipe in place. Brass cap is slipped over lamp pipe and sets on top of column. Some sanding may need to be done to get a good fit. Slide the brass check ring over the lamp pipe and secure in place with washer and hexnut (Fig. 3-98).
6. Cut copper tubing to desired length. A 27-inch length of copper was used for this lamp. Add a sleeve cut from a copper coupling to one end of the copper tubing. Slide tubing over lamp pipe. The sleeve should fit inside brass check ring (Fig. 3-99).

Fig. 3-99. Copper tubing with a 1-inch interior diameter is slid over the lamp pipe. A copper cap and check ring are added before socket and harp.

Fig. 3-100. The electrical cord comes out a small hole near the base of the lamp.

7. Drill a ⅜-inch hole through the copper cap and slide over copper tubing and lamp pipe.
8. Add brass check ring if desired and secure in place with round or hex-shaped nut.
9. Add harp and socket base.
10. Drill a ¼-inch hole through the base of column for the electrical cord outlet. ¼-inch hole should come out at a point below the lamp pipe in the countersunk hole (Fig. 3-100).
11. Run the electrical cord through the base and lamp pipe. Strip away the insulation and attach the wires to the socket terminals. Push the socket into place.
12. Add an electrical plug.
13. Sand and paint or stain wood base. Let dry.
14. Add harp, light bulb, desired shade and finial.

Oak Table Lamp

Fig. 3-101. A salvaged table top and some ingenuity turn oak, copper and turned wood into a table lamp.

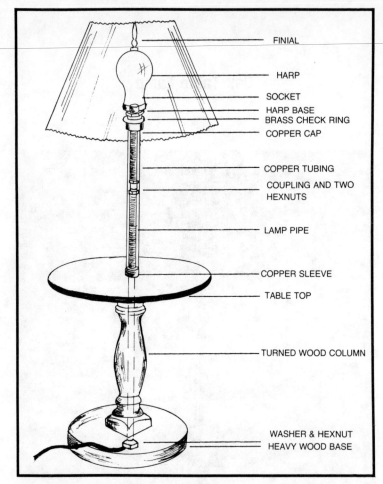

FINIAL

HARP

SOCKET

HARP BASE
BRASS CHECK RING

COPPER CAP

COPPER TUBING

COUPLING AND TWO
HEXNUTS

LAMP PIPE

COPPER SLEEVE

TABLE TOP

TURNED WOOD COLUMN

WASHER & HEXNUT
HEAVY WOOD BASE

Fig. 3-102. Parts of a table lamp assembled.

Some small tables can be converted into attractive lamps with a
minimum of work. The table lamp shown here (Fig. 3-101) is created
from an old oak table top that was salvaged from a trash can. The
table top was painted red when found. After sanding away the red
paint, I found an oak table top.

This lamp is made from pieces of oak and a turned wood column
purchased from a lumber yard. It's possible to find unfinished tables
at a reasonable cost in some stores. Look for tables that have a
column supporting the table top. The tables you use for this type of
lamp construction should be heavy enough to support the copper
tubing and lamp construction.

Before purchasing a table, find out how the column and legs are attached to the table. Keep in mind you have to drill through the length of the column; and if a bolt of some sort is in the column center, you can hold the table top in place and drill through it. If you can remove the bolt, you might be able to use the table because the table top is held to the column and legs by the lamp pipe and hexnuts.

The structure of this lamp is very similar to the wood and copper floor lamp. The only difference is the addition of the table top. Figure 3-102 shows the parts of the table lamp assembled.

Fig. 3-103. A hole drilled part way through the center of the table top helps hold the table together and supports the copper tubing.

MATERIALS

Unfinished, small wood table with column construction
One-inch inside diameter copper tubing
Copper coupling and copper cap
Lamp pipe
Coupling
Socket
Harp assembly
Washers and nuts
Electrical cord and plug
Light bulb, lampshade and finial
Wood finishing materials
Tools for construction

Fig. 3-104. A brass vase cap is used on top of the turned wood to make sure the table sits correctly and helps guide the lamp pipe.

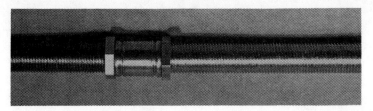

Fig. 3-105. A hole needs to be drilled through the center of the copper cap for the lamp pipe.

CONSTRUCTION STEPS

1. Find the center of the table. Remove the table top from the supporting column, if necessary. Drill a ¾ or ⅝-inch hole through the column using a bit extension. Countersink a 1-inch hole first, if a round base is attached to the column as illustrated (Fig. 3-103).

2. Drill a ⅜-inch hole through the exact center of the table top after it is removed from the column.

3. Insert the lamp pipe through the table and column. Use hexnuts and washers to hold lamp pipe in place as well as the table top (Fig. 3-104).

4. Cut copper tubing to proper length. Twenty inches of tubing was used for this lamp.

5. Cut the needed length of lamp pipe and attach to lamp pipe using coupling and two hexnuts.

6. Drill a ⅜-inch hole through the center of the copper cap and add to copper tubing (Fig. 3-105).

7. Cut a copper coupling in two with a hacksaw to make a sleeve. Slide over copper tubing opposite capped end.

8. Slip copper tubing over the lamp pipe and secure in place with a hexnut and check ring if desired.

9. Attach the harp and socket base to the lamp pipe.

10. Drill a ¼-inch hole for the electrical cord outlet through the side of the column wood base or the electrical cord can pass out the lamp pipe at the bottom of the column. Placement of the electrical cord outlet depends on the structure of the table.

11. Insert the electrical cord through the lamp pipe. Strip away the insulation and attach the bare wires to the socket terminals. Push socket back in place.

12. Add the electrical plug.

13. Sand and stain or paint table. Let dry.

14. Add a harp, light bulb, lampshade and finial.

Turn Almost Anything into a Lamp

By this point you should have a fairly good idea of how to make lamps. It's now just a matter of stimulating your imagination, so you can construct a unique lamp that will fit your own personal needs.

On the next few pages are visual ideas for lamp making. Various objects that could be transformed into decorative and functional lamps are shown (Fig. 4-1). Hopefully, some of the objects will give you ideas that you can use (Fig. 4-2).

WHERE TO GET LAMP-MAKING IDEAS

If someone were to ask me where I get my ideas for the lamps I make, I would respond, "Everywhere I go." Any store or new environment offers lamp-making ideas. It all depends on how you look at different objects and how you answer the question, "Can that become a lamp?"

There is a limit to how many lamps the average person can make. A home only needs so many lamps. If you become an avid lamp-making hobbyist, you'll probably make a few lamps for friends and relatives, as well as meeting your own needs (Fig. 4-3).

Here are a few suggestions for where to look for lamp-making ideas. Swap meets or flea markets are excellent places to go browsing for ideas. At these gatherings you'll find that one person's junk just might be the lamp base you are looking for (Fig. 4-4). Often you can negotiate the price and get a real bargain (Fig. 4-5).

Yard sales are similar to the swap meets and flea markets. The only difference is there isn't as much to choose from (Fig. 4-6). On

Fig. 4-1. Objects that would make unique lamps.

Fig. 4-2. Glassware of all types can be converted into lamps.

occasion you might find an old lamp someone is trying to get rid of. If the price is right, buy the lamp and salvage the parts for your own creations.

Gift shops sell many unusual things (Fig. 4-7) but the bargains are few. Look for close-outs and slightly damaged merchandise to save yourself some money (Fig. 4-8). Of course, if you can afford the prices, buy what you need.

Import shops are about the same as gift shops but specialize in merchandise from China, Japan, India, Mexico and other places

Fig. 4-3. The hub of an old wagon wheel has been converted into a table lamp.

Fig. 4-4. Wine decanter could be converted into a small table lamp.

Fig. 4-5. These bottles would make excellent lamp bases.

around the world (Fig. 4-9). Sometimes you can find great lamp-makng materials at very little cost.

Hardware stores are fascinating places to prowl. It's amazing how many different things are sold in hardware stores and how few people know what the things are. Plumbing fittings and other building materials can be converted into unusual lamps.

SPECIAL CONSTRUCTION PROBLEMS AND SOLUTIONS

At times you'll find an object you would like to convert into a lamp but are not quite sure how to go about it (Fig. 4-10). These ideas might help you overcome some problems you might encounter.

Fig. 4-6. You may find a pitcher at a yard sale that would make an attractive lamp.

Fig. 4-7. Unusual items will make striking lamps.

For example, the opening of the object is too large for a vase cap and you are not quite sure how to support the lamp pipe which holds the light socket and shade (Fig. 4-11).

There are three possible solutions to the problem. One approach you might want to try is using a lamp base within the object. You can attach the proper length of lamp pipe to a heavy wood base that fits inside the object you are converting to a lamp. The base should be heavy so that it does not move around.

Another approach to the problem is using quick-drying plaster-of-paris to hold the lamp pipe within the object. If using plaster-of-paris, you must drill through the object for the lamp cord and then wire the socket in place. The final step is to hold the lamp pipe in place and fill the object with the mixture of plaster-of-paris. A

Fig. 4-8. Look in gift shops for bargains.

Fig. 4-9. Import shops offer oriental items that will make attractive lamps.

Fig. 4-10. Interesting wood from a mining operation has been turned into a table lamp.

two or three-inch depth of plaster-of-paris should be plenty to support the lamp pipe.

Instead of using plaster-of-paris you may want to use modeling clay to support the lamp pipe. This will be less permanent than using the plaster.

One last approach to the problem is using the plastic foam that is often used in packaging and can be purchased in craft shops. The material is rigid but soft so that sharp objects can be pushed through. The plastic foam is not too attractive by itself, so if the material shows in your lamp construction you may want to cover it with a decorative material that can be cloth or even the self-adhesive contact papers.

Another problem you may find in your lamp construction is converting objects you do not wish to drill through. This is one of the easiest of problems to overcome.

You'll need a decorative base and bent figurine lamp pipe (Fig. 4-12). In construction of a lamp of this sort the lamp pipe runs from

Fig. 4-11. The mouth of this vase may be too large for a vase cap.

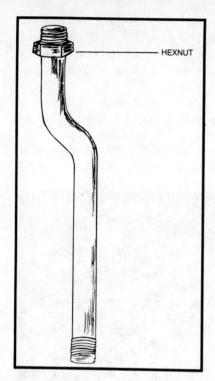

HEXNUT

Fig. 4-12. Bent figurine lamp pipe.

the base behind the decorative object and then bends back over the object (Fig. 4-13).

You may want to build a lamp of this sort and just place the decorative object on the base. That way when you tire of the object that is in the limelight, you just replace it with something different. Figurine lamp pipe can be purchased in an adjustable form from 10 to 15 inches and from 15 to 25 inches.

IDEAS TO TRY

Here's a list of 20 objects that could be converted into lamps:

1. Colorful boxes
2. Colorful tile on wood
3. Kitchen utensil, such as a copper tea kettle
4. Picture frames of wood or metal
5. Candlestick holders
6. Masonry bricks
7. Plumbing pipe of copper or plastic
8. Clay pipe
9. Dolls
10. Duck decoys

11. Fabric on wood
12. Stacked cans
13. Antiques of all sorts
14. Mirrors on wood
15. A table clock
16. Waste paper basket
17. Stacked rolls of ribbon
18. Wrapped yarn on wood
19. Large sea shells
20. Bird cage

The remaining pages of this chapter are pictures of different objects taken from gift shops, lumber supply, furniture stores and so on. Look at each object and decide how the object could be transformed into a decorative lamp. Some of the objects are fairly large

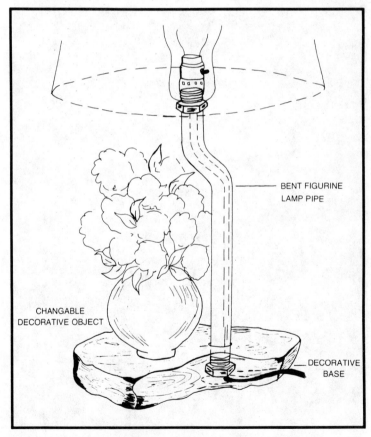

Fig. 4-13. Decorative lamp constructed with bent figurine lamp pipe.

Fig. 4-14. A striped vase may go best with your decor.

while others are small. Size should always be considered before turning an object into a lamp.

Hopefully, your imagination will be stimulated and you'll build your own unique lamps.

Fig. 4-15. A vase with a small mouth would be easy to convert into a lamp.

Fig. 4-16. Ceramics of all types can be made into lamps.

Fig. 4-17. Vases with an unusual pattern would make striking lamps.

Fig. 4-18. This centerpiece of driftwood would make an unusual lamp.

Fig. 4-19. Using the wood base, lamp pipe could run behind the eagle without damaging it.

Fig. 4-20. Animal figurines make distinctive lamps.

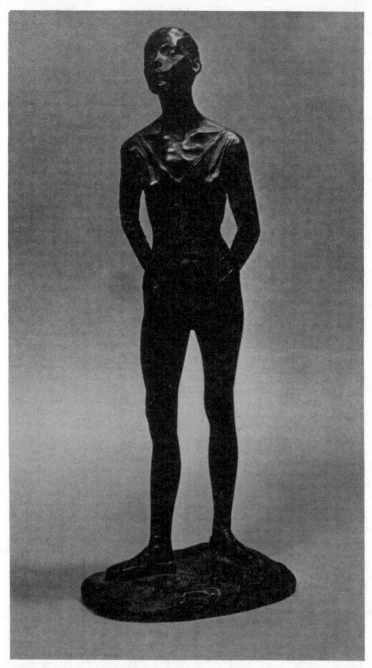

Fig. 4-21. Tall, narrow figurines can be turned into lamps by using bent figurine lamp pipe and bases.

Fig. 4-22. Antiques can add decorative lamps to your home.

Fig. 4-23. This wooden vase would make a striking table lamp.

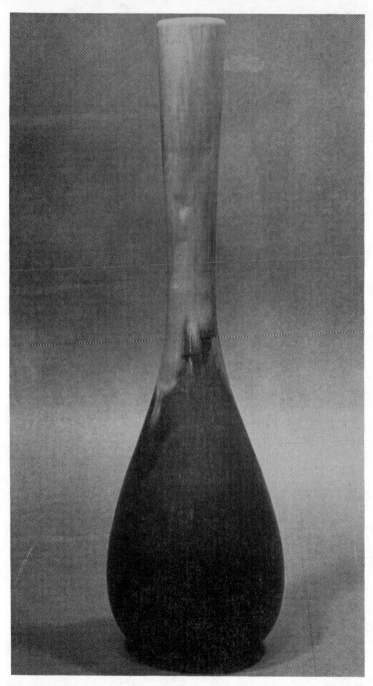

Fig. 4-24. This vase would make a tall, slender lamp.

Fig. 4-25. Packing barrels could be transformed into a table and lamp.

Fig. 4-26. The large milk can could be converted into a floor lamp.

Fig. 4-27. Small, decorative stove could be turned into a table and lamp.

Fig. 4-28. Metal plant stands can be converted into floor lamps using special light bulbs that stimulate plant growth.

Fig. 4-29. Wood objects are easily converted into lamps.

Fig. 4-30. Cookie jar makes a fun lamp for a child's room.

Fig. 4-31. Baskets make attractive lamps when filled with artificial flowers.

Fig. 4-32. This sculpture could make an elegant lamp.

195

Fig. 4-33. A figurine planter is a good idea to try.

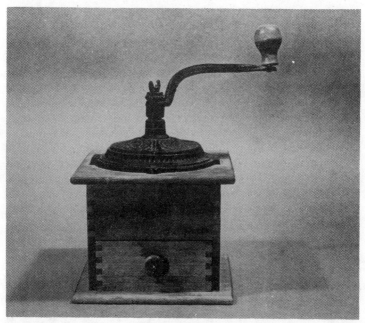

Fig. 4-35. Coffee grinder could be made into a lamp using bent lamp pipe from a wood base.

196

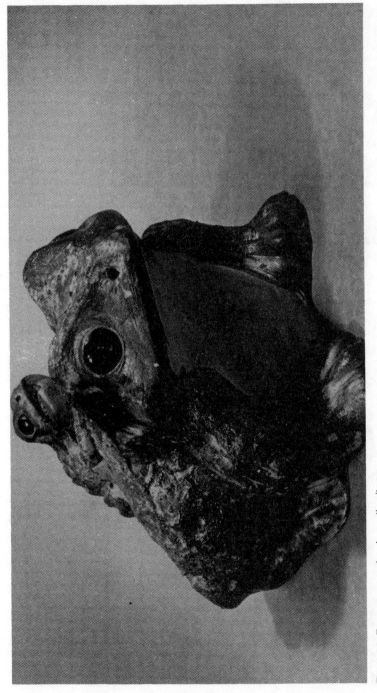

Fig. 4-34. Frogs are popular decorative items.

197

Fig. 4-36. This pelican would make a pleasing lamp for a child's room.

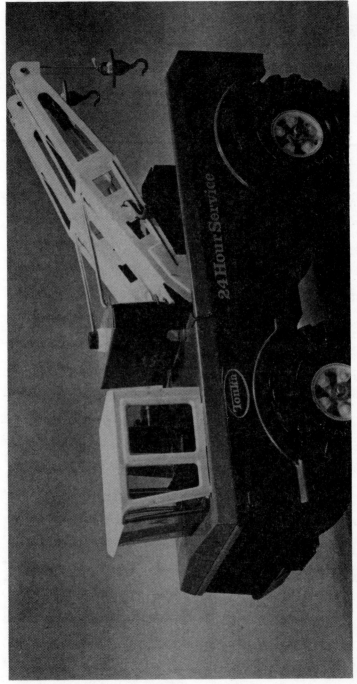

Fig. 4-37. When the children quit playing with their toys, you might consider turning some of their things into lamps. The wheels on this truck would have to be glued to keep from moving.

Lampshades: The Final Touch 5

Choosing a lampshade for your lighting creations can be a troublesome experience. The right lampshade can enhance the beauty and uniqueness of your lamp. The wrong lampshade can hinder the usefulness of a lamp or make the lamp unappealing.

Lampshades come in all sizes, shapes, and colors (Fig. 5-1). They can be made of plastic, parchment, fine fabrics and combinations of materials. Some of the materials are easy to keep clean while others will require brushing, vacuuming, or even washing to maintain their attractive appearance.

TRY THE SHADE ON

The easiest way to find a shade is to take your finished lamp to the nearest store that sells a vast selection of lampshades. That way you can try shades, as you would a hat, to see which one is most fitting.

The shape of the lamp will dictate the type of lampshade you need. Should the shade be oval, cone or tiffany shaped? That depends on the type of lamp you have constructed and what truly appeals to you.

Another consideration before selecting a lampshade is the way the light is reflected from the shade when the lamp's bulb is turned on. Lampshades, depending on their shapes, distribute light differently. Some may direct light towards the ceiling leaving an interesting lighting design that may enhance the appearance of your room.

Fig. 5-1. Lamp shades come in all sizes, shapes, and colors.

Other shades will direct the light below the shade, lighting a specific area around the lamp. Other shades may emit light above, below and through the shade.

Keep in mind that lamps provide light, but during the day they are nothing more than decorative objects. So, a lampshade must not only be appealing when the light is on, but also as it stands by itself.

Small lampshades will have a built-in harp, one that slides over the light bulb. The little attachment is a butterfly clip. Be sure not to purchase a lampshade with a built-in harp if your lamp has its own harp system (Fig. 5-2).

Other lampshades are made with a center supporting ring and three wires that hold the supporting ring in place. These attachments are generally found on the large lampshades (Fig. 5-3).

The supporting ring for large lampshades can be near the top of the shade or it can be somewhere below the top of the shade. The placement of the ring can make a difference as to how the lampshade will fit.

Some lamps may seem too high for the lamps. They can be lowered by changing the harp on the lamp. The detachable harp assemblies come in a selection of sizes. So, if the shade seems to fit

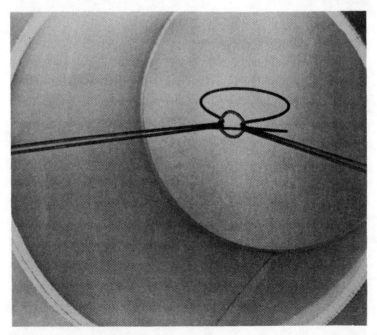

Fig. 5-2. The built-in butterfly clip of this shade means no harp is needed. The clip slides over the socket's light bulb.

Fig. 5-3. A spider and center supporting ring of a lampshade. This type of shade is used on large lamps.

too high on the lamp, try lowering the shade by using a different harp.

The lampshade may seem to be too low on some lamps. This time try a larger harp to raise the shade. Sometimes you can find special attachments that screw onto the top of the harp assembly. This will raise the shade a little bit.

MAKE YOUR OWN LAMPSHADE

It is possible to make your own unique lampshades. If you are good with sewing and have the patience to cut strange-fitting shapes from parchment, by all means try making your own lampshades.

The problem will be finding the necessary wire shapes for making lampshades. Some lampshade stores may sell the wire frames that are the heart of the shade. But before you can make a lampshade you still have to know which shape is the most desirable on the lamp you have built.

To find this out you have to try on several shades at a lampshade store. You may find one that you like at the store to give you ideas.

To get the hang of lampshade making, you might first try covering an old shade that you already have with new material. All you have to do is cement a new cover over the old one (Fig. 5-4).

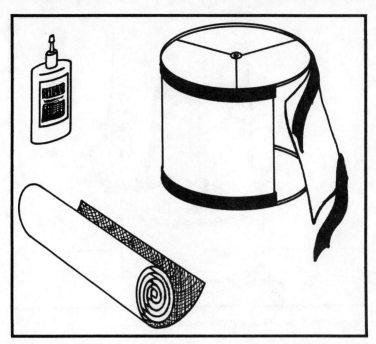

Fig. 5-4. Glue a new cover on an old shade and you have an easy, brand new shade.

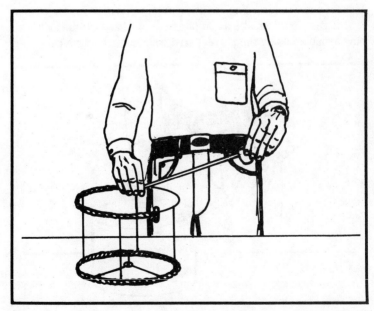

Fig. 5-5. Wrap the frame in bias tape, holding it in place with a paper clip as you work.

Fig. 5-6. Wrap the new shade around the frame.

First, mix the glue with water so it easily spreads over the old shade. Align the new shade over the old one. Be sure to squeeze out bubbles and wrinkles. You can add a pretty trim to cover the edges.

If you want to make a completely new shade for the lamp but have trouble finding the correct size frame, remove the old cover

Fig. 5-7. Cover the edges with fancy fabric.

from a shade that fits and use that frame. You can even use the old covering as a blueprint for the new one, and you won't have the trouble of gluing.

Before you add the new material, wrap the frame in bias tape. It can be held in place while you work with a paperclip (Fig. 5-5). Sew the two ends together where they overlap.

Use clips again as you wrap the new shade around the frame (Fig. 5-6). You will have a one-inch overlap. Cement the cover to the edges and hold it in place with clips until set.

Hide the edges with a fancy trim. Be careful when gluing trim to the shade. Be sure to overlap it on the inside to hide bias tape encircling the frame (Fig. 5-7).

Additional Reading

1. Cox, Dorothy. *The Modern Lampshade Book*. London: G. Bell and Sons Ltd., 1973
   Lampshade making from a British point of view with photographs and diagrams.
2. DeCristoforo, R. J. *Handtool Handbook for Woodworking*. Tucson, Arizona: H. P. Books, 1977
   A well-illustrated guide to many tools, some you will need in your lamp construction.
3. Fishburn, Angela. *Making Lampshades*. New York: Drake Publishers, Inc., 1975
   Lampshade making with another British point of view; photographs and diagrams.
4. Menke, H. A. *28 Table Lamp Projects*. Bloomington, Illinois: McKnight and McKnight Publishing, 1953.
   Photos and diagrams for wood workers only.
5. Montagna, Pier. *How to Make Lamps and Lampshades*. New York: Key Publishing, 1963
   A diagrams-only book that includes drapery and curtain making.
6. Murphy, Bruce W. and Ana G. Lopo. *Lampmaking*. New York: Drake Publishing, 1976.
   Step by step instruction to making many popular table lamps and some unusual ceiling lights.
   Many photographs and diagrams.
7. *Sunset* Magazine Editors. *Lighting Your Home*. Menlo Park, California: Lane Publishing, 1963
   Nothing on lamps but an illustrated guide to lighting your home.

Index